SCIENCE FAIR PROJECTS

Energy

Bob Bonnet & Dan Keen
Illustrated by Alex Pang

Sterling Publishing Co., Inc.
New York

This book is dedicated to our first grandchildren,
Carly Michelle and Michaela Elizabeth.
Save some energy for science.

Edited by Claire Bazinet

Library of Congress Cataloging-in-Publication Data

Bonnet, Robert L.
    Science fair projects : energy / Bob Bonnet & Dan Keen ; illustrated by Alex Pang.
        p.   cm.
    Includes index.
    ISBN 0-8069-9793-1
    1. Force and energy — Study and teaching — Activity programs. 2. Science projects
— Handbooks, manuals, etc. I. Keen, Dan. II. Title.
    QC73.6.B66   1997
    531'.6'078–dc21   97-33088
                                                                                            CIP

10 9 8 7 6 5 4 3 2 1

Published by Sterling Publishing Company, Inc.
387 Park Avenue South, New York, N.Y. 10016
© 1997 by Bob Bonnet and Dan Keen
Distributed in Canada by Sterling Publishing
℅ Canadian Manda Group, One Atlantic Avenue, Suite 105
Toronto, Ontario, Canada M6K 3E7
Distributed in Great Britain and Europe by Cassell PLC
Wellington House, 125 Strand, London WC2R 0BB, England
Distributed in Australia by Capricorn Link (Australia) Pty Ltd.
P.O. Box 6651, Baulkham Hills, Business Centre, NSW 2153, Australia
Manufactured in the United States of America
All rights reserved

Sterling ISBN 0-8069-9793-1

CONTENTS

A Note to the Parent

All children are scientists, constantly searching for explanations to their questions about the world around them. Their quest should be enjoyable, interesting, and thought-provoking...as science is. This is the concept that the writers wish to convey in this book. In addition to presenting many valuable and useful scientific ideas and learning techniques, the book is designed to entice the young child with the excitement and fun of scientific investigation.

ENERGY

Welcome to the fascinating world of energy! This book explores projects in energy and the physics of energy. The term "energy" is difficult to give a meaning to, since it is found in many forms and is closely linked to "forces" (magnetism, gravity, wind, etc.). Physicists define energy as the ability to do work, and they define "work" as the ability to move an object over a distance.

Forms of energy include solar, mechanical, chemical, electrical, moving fluids (both gases and liquids, etc.), heat, light, sound, pressure, thermal, nuclear, electromagnetic waves, respiration (living things get energy from foods, and muscles do work), and the forces of weather, gravity, and magnetism.

Energy can be transferred from one object to another; a rolling marble strikes a stationary marble and causes it to start rolling. Energy can be converted from one form to another, such as light energy to heat energy. Albert Einstein is known for the formula $E = mc^2$ he put forth in 1905, stating that matter can be changed into energy and energy into matter.

Energy is said to be either "kinetic" or "potential." Potential energy is "stored-up" energy—something that has the ability to do work. Kinetic energy is the energy of movement, when work is actually being done. Potential energy can be converted into kinetic energy, and vice versa. Energy from sunlight is stored in trees (potential energy), which can be burned in a fireplace to produce heat (kinetic energy). Roll a rock up a hill (using kinetic energy), and set it on the hilltop (potential energy), where, because of gravity, it has the potential to do work (when it falls).

SCIENCE FAIR PROJECTS

The material in this book is presented in a light and interesting fashion. For example, the concept of measurement can be demonstrated by teaching precise measuring in inches or centimeters (equivalents in this book are approximate), or by having a child stretch his or her arms around a tree trunk and asking, "Are all children's reaches the same?" We present science in a way that does not seem like science.

The scientific concepts introduced here will help the young student to understand more advanced scientific principles later. Projects will develop those science skills needed in our ever-increasing complex society: skills such as classifying objects, making measured observations, thinking clearly, and recording data accurately. Values are dealt with in a general way. One should never harm any living thing just for the sake of it. Respect for life should be fundamental. Disruption of natural processes should not occur thoughtlessly and unnecessarily. Interference with ecological systems should always be avoided.

The activities presented in this book target third- through fifth-grade students. The materials needed to do most of the activities are commonly found around the home or are easily available at minimal cost.

Because safety is and must always be the first consideration, we recommend that all activities be done under adult supervision. Even seemingly harmless objects can become a hazard under certain circumstances. For example, a bowling ball can be a danger if it is allowed to fall on a child's foot.

There are many benefits in store for a child who chooses to do a science project. It motivates the child to learn. Such an activity helps develop thinking skills; it prompts a child to question, and learn how to solve problems. In these activities, the child is asked to make observations using all the senses and to record those observations accurately and honestly. Quantitative measurements of distance, size, and volume must be made. Students may find a subject so interesting that, after the project is completed, they will want to do more investigation on their own. Spin-off interests can develop, too. In doing a science project about energy conservation, while using a computer to record data, a child may discover an interest in computers.

The authors recommend that parents take an active interest in their child's science project. Apart from the safety aspect, when a parent is involved, contact time between the parent and child increases. Such quality time strengthens relationships as well as the child's self-esteem. Working on a project is an experience that can be shared. An involved parent is telling the child that he or she believes that education is important. Parents need to support the academic learning process at least as much as they support Little League, music lessons, or any other growth activity

Parents should take the time to help the student in reading, understanding, and completing these educational and fun projects. Adults can be an invaluable resource that the child draws upon for information, as older people are given the opportunity to share their own learning and life experiences. Transportation may be helpful and appreciated, such as taking the child to a library or other places for research. One student in our school, doing a project on insects, was taken by his parents to the Mosquito Commission Laboratory, where he was able to talk with professionals in the field.

Many projects in this book have been designed as "around-you science," in contrast to "book science." By "around-you science" we mean doing a science project right where you are—in your home, your neighborhood, your school. Getting ideas for a science fair project can even begin right at your feet. What happens when you kick a rock? Why are darker colors worn in the wintertime? Is there energy in your body? How did it get there? What can you do to save energy in your home or school? Get excited with your child about the world around us!

Clear and creative thought is a primary goal for the young scientific mind. This book will help prepare a young person for future involvement and satisfying experiences in the field of science.

Bob Bonnet & Dan Keen

Project 1

SHRINKING CUBES

Changing the sun's light into heat energy

Imagine a sunny day at a picnic. You pour a glass of cola soda to drink. Your friend fills a glass with a lemon-lime soda he likes. You both take one ice cube. Which ice cube will last longer?

Sunlight turns into heat energy. Things that are dark in color absorb more light energy than those that are lighter, so they become hotter. Will the darker soda collect more sunlight and melt the cube faster?

Take two same-size clear glasses, fill one with a clear or light-colored soda and one with a dark-

You need
- 2 same-size clear drinking glasses
- clear-colored soda drink
- dark-colored soda drink
- a table by a sunny window
- 2 same-size ice cubes
- a dark room

colored drink. Fill each glass to the same height, not quite to the top. Place the glasses in a sunny window for a half hour. Then, take two ice cubes of equal size and drop one into each glass. Which of the two ice cubes lasts longer? Why?

In this project, an assumption is made. We are assuming (we "think") that the kind of soda itself (flavor, sweetness) does not affect the melting of the ice cubes. To prove that our assumption is correct, do the experiment again. This time, set both glasses of soda in a dark room instead of in the sun. If both ice cubes take the same amount of time to melt, then the sodas had an equal effect on the ice cubes, and our assumption is correct.

Test out other drinks: orange juice, red punch, lemonade, ginger ale. Try carbonated/noncarbonated, diet (sugar substitute)/high sugar, with/without solids (pulp), etc.

What else about a drink might affect the melting speed of ice cubes? How can you find out if it does?

Project 2

FROSTY'S SUNSCREEN

Warding off the sun's heating rays

It's fun to build a snowman and have it stand guard in your yard all winter long. But rising temperatures and the sun's heat are not kind to snowmen. It can quickly make them melt away.

Will putting a "hat" or kerchief on your snowman's head help shade him from the sun and keep him around longer?

You need
• a sunny day with snow on the ground
• large black plastic bag
• large white plastic bag

On a sunny day when there is snow on the ground, build two identical snowmen. Fold a large black plastic (trash) bag into a kerchief or hat and place or tie it on the head of one snowman. You might need to use snow or small twigs to help hold it in place.

Fold a large white plastic bag as you did the black and place it on the head of the other snowman. Again, keep it in place by tying or using snow or small twigs.

As the day goes by, check each snowman to see if there has been any melting. If so, which one's head shows the most melting?

Plastic bags often come in other colors—blue, red, and green, for example. Would using these colors as hats make any difference in keeping a snowman around longer? Would using no kerchief make a difference? (If there's not enough snow available to make several large, whole snowmen, just make large snowball "heads" and wrap same-size sections of the different-colored bags on them for this experiment.)

Project 3
GETTING STEAMED
Water vapor put to work

Steam is water changed into a gas by heat energy. We use the energy of steam to do many things. Steam has been used to power boats and trains. Steam turbines generate electricity when steam pressure pushes against blades or paddles connected to a shaft and turns the shaft. On the other end of the shaft is an electrical generator.

Get a Pyrex beaker, a one-hole rubber stopper, and a glass tube with a 90-degree, or right-angle, bend. These items can be purchased inexpensively at a science store or borrowed from your science teacher at school.

Never work around a hot stove without an adult with you. Be very careful! The stove burner, the beaker, and the escaping steam will be hot. Do not touch them!

Pour some water into the beaker. Insert the rubber stopper in the top; then ask an adult to gently push one end of the bent glass tube through the hole in the stopper.

Set the beaker on the burner of a stove or a hot plate and turn it on high heat. Open the pages slightly of a tall hard-bound book and stand it next to (but not too close to) the burner. Lay a toy pinwheel on a stick on top of the book and extend it out so that the pinwheel paddles are in the path of the escaping steam from the tube. Do you think heat energy is being changed into mechanical energy?

Project 4

HOT STUFF

Heat energy from decomposition

Heat energy is given off when organic things (material that was once alive) decay. Many people who plant gardens have "compost piles" to make fertilizer for feeding the garden. A compost pile is a small area, often boxed, filled with dead or dying plant and animal leavings such as peels and scraps from the kitchen, fallen leaves, grass clippings, manure, hay, and other things that rot. The material is stacked and allowed to decay for months, as it turns into rich fertilizer. As it decays, heat is given off.

You need
- freshly mowed grass clippings
- a warm, sunny day
- lawn rake
- clock or watch

When your lawn or your neighbor's lawn is mowed, gather some grass clippings by using a lawn rake. Make a pile of grass clippings 1 foot (30 cm) high and about 1 foot (30 cm) in diameter. Place the pile on the lawn in a bright, sunny spot. Let it sit in the sunlight.

After two hours, use the rake to make another pile of grass clippings and place it next to the first one. Both piles should be the same size. Wait ten minutes. Then push one hand into the middle of each pile. Does the inside of one pile feel warmer than the other? If so, which pile feels warmer, the one you just raked or the one that has been sitting in the sunlight for two hours?

Do you think grass clippings can be used to make a good habitat or nest for some animals?

Project 5
BOTTLED GAS
Stored chemical energy (CO₂) in soda

Carbon dioxide (CO_2) is a colorless gas. Humans and animals breathe out carbon dioxide. It is also formed when things made of carbon, such as charcoal, wood, and coal, are burned.

Energy is used by the food industry to dissolve carbon dioxide into water; this adds the "fizz" to carbonated soda drinks. As long as the soda bottle remains unopened or the opened soda is kept tightly capped, the carbon dioxide stays dissolved. But as soon as the cap is taken off the bottle, the carbon dioxide starts to expand and escape (this is chemical energy).

What happens when you pour a carbonated soda into a glass slowly? What happens when you pour fast? The release of carbon dioxide is what makes the bubbles in soda, and gives it a foamy head. We can show that there is energy being released by making the expanding carbon dioxide do work.

First, stretch a balloon several times in all directions. Blow it up as big as it will go, then let all the air out. Doing this will make the balloon easier to inflate.

Open a bottle of carbonated soda (read the label if you aren't sure whether the drink is carbonated). Remove the cap and stretch the opening of the balloon over the mouth of the bottle. Carefully, shake the bottle to release carbon dioxide from the soda. What happens to the balloon?

Do you have an unopened bottle of soda that has been stored for a long time? Put the balloon over its mouth when you do open it. Does the balloon inflate? What does that tell you about the CO_2 in the soda, and the plastic container or tightness of its cap?

You need
- balloon
- bottle of carbonated soda

13

Project 6

ROLLING STOCK

Potential energy, mass, and gravity

Energy used to move an object up to a height is stored in the object as "potential energy" because gravity pulls downward on the object and will cause it to move. If two objects are raised to the same height, which has more energy stored in it (required more energy to move), the lighter object (less mass) or the heavier one (more mass)?

Stack several books on the floor, making two piles the same height, about 1 foot (30 cm) tall. Make two ramps by propping one end of each long board up on a stack. Shelf boards work well if you have them; if not, have an adult help you find two same-size boards, or cut two boards from a section of plywood.

> **You need**
> - 2 two-liter plastic soda bottles
> - books
> - ruler
> - 2 boards, about 1 × 4 feet (30 × 120 cm)
> - water
> - an adult

Fill a plastic two-liter soda bottle with water and screw the cap on tightly. Screw the cap onto another, empty, plastic two-liter soda bottle. Lift both bottles to the top of the ramps, laying them on their sides, and hold them. Then let go of both of them at the same time. Which one travels farther? The one that travels farther had more potential energy, and therefore also took more energy to move to the top of the ramp.

The bottle that travels farther also has more "momentum." Momentum is a force that moves an object. It is the product of mass times velocity. The bottle filled with water has more mass than the empty one. Now, why do you think it is hard to stop a moving train quickly?

A ramp is an "inclined plane," a type of simple machine. Research inclined planes.

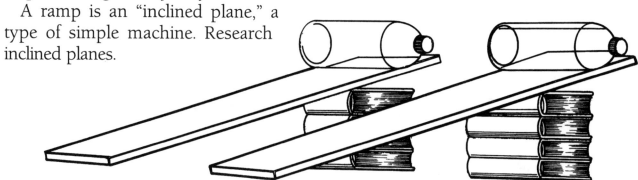

Project 7

STORMY WEATHER

Detecting the energy release of storms

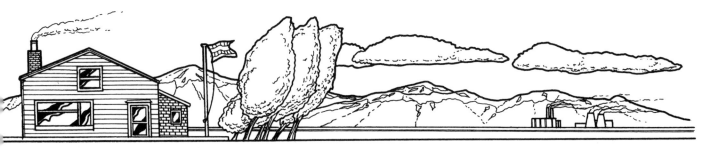

Tremendous amounts of energy are released every minute around the world by the Earth's weather system. Lightning,, wind, hurricanes, and tornadoes are powerful energy producers. It is said that lightning strikes somewhere on Earth 100 times each second! A lightning bolt is thought to release as much as 100 million volts of electricity, with the bolt reaching a temperature as high as 50,000 degrees Fahrenheit (27,760 Celsius).

Next time it storms, look out your windows.* Make a list of evidence that energy is being released by the storm. Remember, energy "works" (the ability to move something over a distance). So, what do you see: trees moving, leaves stirring, the flag and rope on a flagpole whipping around, sand blowing, a clothes line jiggling, a can rolling noisily down the street, paper flying through the air? Is smoke from chimneys rising straight up, or bending or scattering? Are there fierce-looking waves on a large nearby lake? Is sea water spraying from the tops of rough ocean waves?

If it is raining, is the rain falling straight down or at an angle? What is happening when the rain hits the ground? Is a heavy rain causing streams down streets and across yards? Is there evidence of erosion—soil being pushed by the moving water?

Open a window a bit and listen. Write down the sounds of energy release. Do you hear the wailing of the wind? If it is a thunderstorm, do you see lightning and hear the crash of thunder that follows? Using your AM radio, can you detect the crackle and static of radio frequency energy released by the lightning?

*Storms can be dangerous. Make your observations from the safety and comfort of your home. If lightning is *nearby*, do not use the telephone, and move away from windows.

Project 8

BRICK TRICK

Transfer of heat energy in a solid

Heat energy can be transferred, or move *through* an object or *from* one object to another.

Lay two empty small-size (pint) milk cartons on their side, with the spout openings facing upward. With scissors, carefully cut the top side off each carton. The cartons will serve as molds to make two bricks.

First, using the cartons as measuring containers, fill one and a half pint cartons with sand and pour it into an old bucket or paint can. Add 6 ounces of liquid white glue and 2 ounces of water. Mix thoroughly. Then spoon the mixture into an old shirt or a large piece of cheesecloth, and squeeze out any excess water. Place the mixture into each milk-carton mold. In each one, push a pencil halfway into the brick, near one end, and leave it there.

Place the bricks in a sunny window for a few days, until they harden. Roll the pencils that are in the bricks between your fingers a few times as the bricks dry, so the pencils will be easier to remove later. When the bricks are dry and hard, take the pencils out of the bricks. Put a thermometer in each hole left by the pencils.

In a room that has a sunny window, place one brick near the

You need
- 2 small-size milk cartons
- an old bucket or paint can
- an old shirt or cheesecloth
- sand
- water
- liquid white glue
- a tablespoon or scoop
- 2 pencils
- 2 thermometers
- cardboard, about 1 foot (30 cm) square
- scissors
- a sunny window
- wooden paint stirrer or other stick
- paper
- clock or watch

window, where it can get sunlight. Position it so that the end that has the thermometer stuck in it is away from the window. Cut a piece of cardboard to fit over the brick, making a sunshield, so that the front half of the brick is in sunlight but the back half is in shade. Place the other brick on a table in the same room, but away from the sunlight.

Read and write down the temperatures showing on both thermometers. Every five minutes, read and write down the temperatures again. After one hour, compare the temperatures you recorded for both bricks. Did the one in the sunny window show a warmer temperature? Did heat from the sunny side of the brick travel

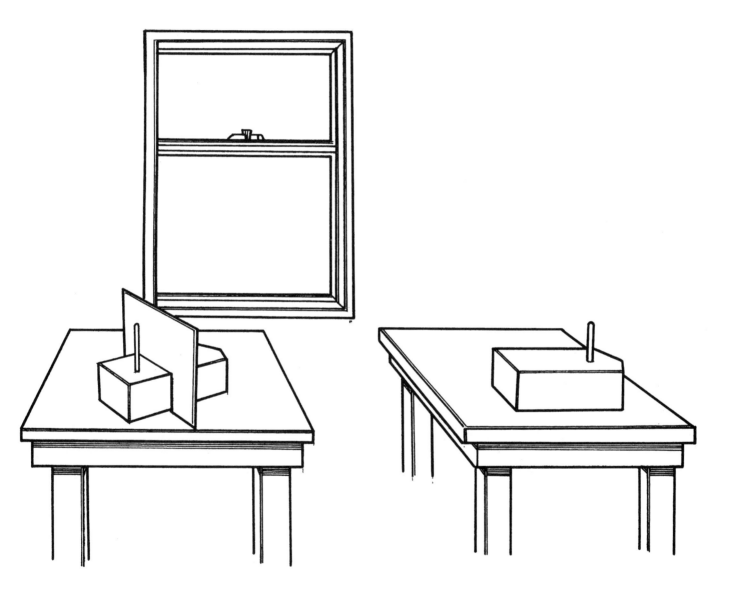

through the brick to the other end? What was the "rate of heat transfer," that is, how fast did the heat move through the brick (*one* degree every five minutes, *two* degrees every five minutes, *three* degrees every five minutes...)?

Project 9

SAILS ALOFT

Using wind energy to power a boat

From mankind's early days, sails have been used on boats to harness the energy of the wind. Let's make small sailboats, using quart-size milk cartons, and experiment with different shapes and sizes of sails.

Lay an empty quart milk carton on its side, with the spout-opening upward. With scissors, cut off the top half of the carton lengthwise to make a boat.

Near the front (pointed end), place a small mound of modeling clay. To make a mast, push the eraser end of a pencil into the clay. A small amount of clay may be needed near the back of the boat to keep the boat balanced. Tape a 1-foot-long (30 cm) piece of string onto the back of the boat so it will drag in the water (this will help hold the boat on course).

Cut a sail out of a piece of paper and tape it to the pencil mast. You may need tape or thread to hold the bottom ends of the paper to the sides of the boat, keeping the sail tight in strong winds. Make several boats using sails of different sizes and shapes.

Find a place outdoors—a small lake, shallow pond, wading pool, public fountain—where you can sail your boat. Have an adult with you for safety around water. Which sail design do you think will make the boats go fastest? Test your sail design.

At the library, research "sailboats" and try different designs on your boats.

You need
- stiff paper
- thread
- pencils
- modeling clay
- string
- scissors
- quart milk cartons
- adhesive tape
- body of shallow water
- an adult

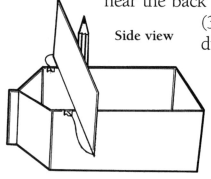
Side view

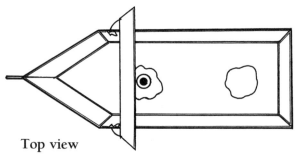
Top view

Project 10

SALT OR NOT?

Comparing solar energy storage in salt and fresh water

Compared to air, water is slow to change temperature. If the weather has been hot for a few days and the water in a swimming pool is warm, one night of cooler temperatures will not change the temperature in the pool very much. It will still be almost as warm the next day.

Does the ability of water to hold the heat energy it has collected differ if the water is salt water or fresh water? Does a saltwater lake cool differently than a freshwater lake when the sun sets?

Fill two 2-liter soda bottles with equally hot water from your kitchen sink (let it run a bit until you get a constant temperature). Add eight teaspoons of salt to one bottle. Stir to dissolve the salt thoroughly.

Instead of screwing the caps on, lightly place a ball of modeling clay over the mouth of each bottle. Carefully push a thermometer into the bottle alongside the clay, so that the bulb of the thermometer is in the water. Make sure you can read the temperature on the thermometer, then press the clay against the thermometer to hold it in place. Do this to both bottles.

Every ten minutes, read the thermometers and write down the temperature readings. After two hours, compare the temperatures you recorded. Did they both lose heat energy at the same rate?

You need
• salt
• 2 two-liter soda bottles
• 2 thermometers
• modeling clay
• hot tap water
• clock
• paper and pencil

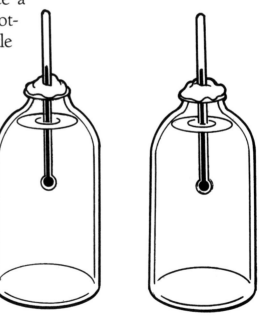

Project 11

THINGS ARE HEATING UP

Graphing solar energy collection in materials

As the sun beats down on the Earth, heat energy is absorbed by everything on the surface. What gathers more of the sun's heat energy: air, water, sand, or stone?

Find four large glasses or, using scissors, carefully cut the top half off four clear 2-liter plastic bottles. (Place the discarded tops in a recyclables trash container.) Stand a ruler upright on a table alongside the container (glass or bottle bottom). Four inches (10 cm) above the table surface, mark the container using a small strip of adhesive tape. Place the top of the tape at the 4-inch height. Do this for all four containers, then write the contents of each container on the tape (air, water, sand or soil, stones). The tape will serve as both a label and the fill-to mark for the containers.

Leave one container empty ("filled" with air). Fill another to the 4-inch mark with water. Fill a third up to the mark with sandy soil. The bulb of each thermometer must be placed, hanging, in the middle of each container, not touching the sides or bottom. For the containers of air and water, suspend the thermometers by placing a section of tape at the top of the thermometer and over a pencil or stick placed across the top of a container. The thermometer bulb should be hanging about 2 inches (5 cm) from the bottom of the container. Carefully push a thermometer down partway into the sandy soil. For the fourth container, hold a thermometer inside the container with one hand so that the bulb

You need
- scissors
- 4 large glasses (or empty 2-liter bottle bottoms)
- a sunny window
- ruler
- masking tape
- water
- sandy soil
- small stones
- 4 thermometers
- 2 pencils or sticks
- clock
- paper and pencil

is 2 inches (5 cm) below the fill line. With the other hand, gently place small stones, about ½ to 1 inch (1–2.5 cm) in diameter, up to the container's fill line.

Set the four containers in a sunny window. After one hour, measure the temperature of each material by reading the thermometers. Write down the temperature readings and compare them.

Take all four containers out of the sunny window and place them somewhere in the room that is out of direct sunlight. Every five minutes for thirty minutes, read the temperatures on the thermometers and write them down in a list. Thirty minutes later, after an hour has passed, record the final temperature readings. Which container lost heat the fastest? Which material continued to give off heat the longest? Was this also the same material that gathered the most heat?

For your project display, make up four simple graphs, see sample for *Air*. Across the top (X-axis) put in the time of the readings (every 5 minutes). List temperatures going down the chart (Y-axis). Then enter your own time–temperature readings of each tested material on its chart.

Project 12

WANT, HELP, NEED

Categorizing home electrical appliances

> **You need**
> • paper and pencil

Many appliances in our homes or apartments save us work and make our lives healthier, happier, and easier. But it also takes energy to run them, usually electrical energy.

Making up a list, search through each room of your home and look for things that use electrical energy (the refrigerator in the kitchen, a hair dryer in the bedroom, lamps in the den, a TV set in the living room). Be sure to include such things as smoke alarms, flashlights, and portable radios, which work off electrical energy stored in batteries.

Once your list is complete, think about each item on your list, and decide if that energy-user is a WANT (you like and want it), a HELP (makes your life easier), or a NEED (necessary in your household).

A need is something that you really must have in order to have a healthy, safe, and working home. If your home is not connected to your city's water system, you probably have a well. In that case, an electric water pump would be necessary to you, supplying water for cooking, cleaning, washing, and personal hygiene.

Consider a help to be something in your home that it is good to have, but that you could do without if you had to. A flashlight would be something you would put in the help category. It's handy to have one in your home in case there is an electric power failure, which might happen during a storm, but day to day you could live without it.

A want is something we have in our home simply because we like it. Usually its purpose is to make our life more enjoyable. A video game may be very entertaining, but it is not necessary to our health or survival.

Some items may fall under a different category for different homes. Although a telephone answering machine is usually just a convenience (a want), if someone is running a business in the home an answering machine may be more of a help or even a necessity, or important business calls could be lost.

Don't forget to check outside your home, too. See if there are any energy-using devices in your yard, such as a swimming-pool pump or security lighting, that should be added to your list.

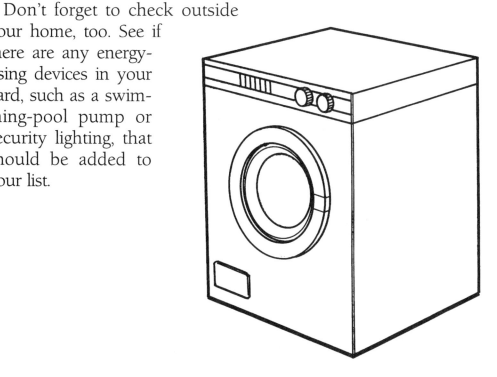

Project 13

YESTERDAY'S ENERGY

Conserving fossil fuels

Fossil fuels are sources of energy that we find within the Earth. We release the energy from such fuels as oil, coal, and natural gas by burning them. These fossil fuels are the remains of animal life and vegetation (energy in the form of trapped

sunlight) that have been within the Earth for millions of years. At the current rate, we are using up our resources of fossil fuels faster than the Earth can make more. Unless we use these fuels more wisely, we will someday run out.

Is your home heated by the burning of fossil fuels? You can save natural gas or heating oil by not letting heat escape through open or drafty doors or windows in cold weather. Can you reduce the need for heating by trapping some of the sun's warming solar energy indoors?

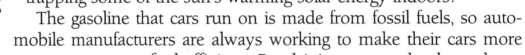

The gasoline that cars run on is made from fossil fuels, so automobile manufacturers are always working to make their cars more fuel-efficient. By driving more slowly and not using cars as much when they don't need to, car owners can help conserve gasoline, too.

How else can we help save fossil fuels? Many electrical power plants make electricity by burning fossil fuels. Are there electrical energy-users you could do *without* to help save electricity?

On a sheet of paper, make a list of appliances that use electricity, such as a hair dryer, electric toothbrush, air conditioner, clock. In a second column beside the appliance, write down ideas for doing the same task without using electricity. In a third column, note whether the energy-saving way would be "a little inconvenient," "very inconvenient," or "a real hardship."

Are there other things to consider about energy usage? You might think of replacing a 100-watt bulb with a 60-watt bulb to save energy. But if the bulb lights the cellar stairway, would it be bright enough to make going down the stairway safe?

Project 14

ONE IF BY LAND

Comparing land and water solar-heat storage

The sun warms our planet. As the Earth turns and night falls, the surface the sun has warmed begins to cool, radiating the heat energy absorbed during the day. What loses heat faster—a body of water or the land near it?

Find a lake, pond, or large swimming pool. (Note: Always have an adult with you for safety when you are working around deep water.)

Tie string to each thermometer. At the end of a sunny day (about 5:00 p.m.), poke a hole 1 to 2 feet deep (30–60 cm) into the ground near a body of water with a long stick. A stake from a game of horseshoes or croquet works best. Lower one thermometer into the hole and tie the other end of the string to the stake. Then, hold the other thermometer in the water. Several minutes later, pull up both thermometers and read and record the temperatures.

You need
- string
- 2 thermometers
- long pointed stick
- body of water
- a sunny day
- pencil and paper
- an adult

Take temperature readings every hour as the sun goes down and record your measurements on a chart. Compare the changes in temperature over time. Which lost heat faster, the land or the water? How do you think this affects the night temperatures of a town located at the edge of a large body of water? Were water and land both heated to the same temperature when you took the first reading?

Project 15

TESTING THE WATERS

An investigation of solar heat distribution

Does the water in a small lake evenly distribute the sun's heat energy, so that the temperature of surface water is the same as the water several feet down? Hypothesize, or guess, which you think will be warmer, the water on the surface of a small lake, the water several feet down, or the water at the edge, along the shoreline.

It is easy to take a lake's temperature near the shoreline. All you need to do is place a thermometer into the water at the edge of the lake. To read the real temperature of the lake's surface and some distance below is a little harder. The thermometers should be placed near the middle of the lake, or at least well out into it, not near the shore. This can be done without going out in a boat or into the water by constructing a small "boat" from wood, with one thermometer hanging below it and dragging a second, floating, thermometer off the back or stern of the boat.

First, find a standard size piece of wood about 6 inches long (15 cm) to serve as the boat that will tow the heat-measuring instruments. Tie a long piece of string to the regular thermometer and fasten the other end to the boat, using a thumbtack or nail. The thermometer should hang down at least 2 feet (60 cm) from the wooden boat. Tie a short piece of string to the thermometer that floats. Fasten the other end of the string to the boat also. Floating thermometers are often used in fish tanks and can be found at aquarium supply stores or pet shops.

Now that you are ready, ask an adult to take you and all your equipment to a nearby pond or lake and stand by to help with this experiment.

You need
- thumbtacks or nails
- 6-inch-long (15 cm) piece of wood (1×2 or 2×4)
- fishing rod and reel
- string
- a thermometer
- a thermometer that floats (an aquarium thermometer)
- metal washers
- a lake or pond
- pencil and paper
- an adult

First, you need to find out the temperature of the lake at the shoreline. Bending carefully on the shore of the lake, place the thermometer in the water. Wait about three minutes to give the thermometer a chance to reach the proper temperature. Then remove the thermometer and immediately read and write down the temperature that it is registering.

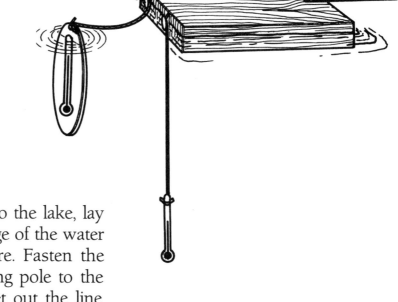

To get the wooden boat out into the lake, lay it securely on the beach at the edge of the water or have your helper hold it there. Fasten the end of a fishing line from a fishing pole to the boat with a thumbtack. Slowly let out the line as you walk around the shore of the lake. (A helper could hold the boat and release it at your signal, when you get into position on the other side.) Carefully reel in the fishing line, dragging the boat and its "instruments" to a spot near the middle of the lake (or at least to a spot where the water is deep). Wait three or four minutes to allow the thermometers to properly change temperature. Then, reel the boat in as quickly as you can, and read the thermometers. The thermometers must be read before they begin to change temperature. The shoreline where you stand to reel in the boat should have sandy or a soft bottom, because quickly dragging the thermometers over a rocky bottom might break them.

Which thermometer read the warmest temperature? Was your hypothesis correct?

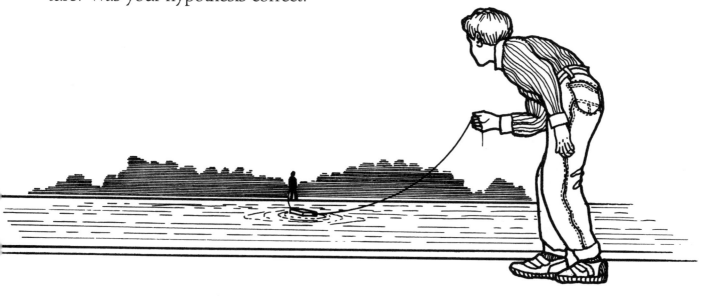

Project 16

OUR TOWN

Transforming and transporting energy

The light that comes from the lamp you read by in the evening is the result of energy changing forms several times and being transported over a great distance.

It all starts at a power plant. Energy from one of several sources is converted into electricity. Some plants burn fossil fuels (coal, oil, or natural gas), converting the solar energy stored in those fuels into heat. The heat is used to make steam that turns the shaft of generators (mechanical energy) to make electricity. Hydroelectric power plants use running water to turn the generators. Nuclear power plants harness radiation energy to make heat for steam generators.

You can show how energy can be changed from one form to another, transported over a distance, and then changed into another form of energy. The network of electric wiring in your community is a perfect example. Build a model town to demonstrate this process.

You need
- miniature 6-volt hobby lamps (bulbs)
- lamp sockets
- hookup wire
- jumper leads with alligator-clip ends
- 6-volt lantern battery with spring-top connectors
- modeling clay
- flat sticks (from ice-cream bars) or strong straws
- glue or tape
- toy buildings used for model-train layouts
- wire cutters or scissors
- screwdriver

Use a 6-volt lantern battery to represent the electric power plant, where one form of energy is turned into another. (In the case of the battery, chemical energy inside it converts to electrical energy.) With hookup wire, connect three miniature (hobby) lamp sockets together.

Glue or tape flat sticks, or strong straws, together to form a cross or "T" shape These will serve as telephone poles. Make several of these "poles." Push each pole into a lump of modeling clay to hold it upright. Using the appropriate tool, cut a small notch in the top of each telephone pole arm. Place the hookup wire in the notches to hold them in place.

Using houses from a model-train or other set (or making your own out of cardboard), position them to form a small town. Put a lamp in each house to light it. The telephone poles should be positioned to run the wires from the battery and to the lamps in each home.

Energy is changed once again when it reaches each lamp. There, it is converted into light energy to illuminate the model homes, as it is in your own.

Schematic Diagram

lamp

6-volt
battery

6
VOLTS

Project 17
POWER RANGER
Measuring home electrical energy usage

Electric power is measured in units called "watts." You've probably heard someone ask for a 40-, or 60-, or 100-watt bulb to change a burned-out light bulb. The number indicates how much electric power the bulb uses to reach full brightness. (Which do you think is brighter, a 60-watt or 100-watt bulb? Which uses more power?)

You need
• access to your home's electric meter
• pencil and paper

Every month, the electric company bills people for the amount of electricity they used. Electrical usage is measured in "kilowatt-hours." One kilowatt equals 1,000 watts. One kilowatt-hour is 1,000 watts of electric power being used for one hour. It takes one kilowatt-hour of energy to operate ten 100-watt light bulbs for one hour.

How much electrical energy does your home use in one day? Find the electric meter for your home (usually outside, where someone from the power company can find and read it easily). The meter's face has dials on it, marked with numbers. The dials, reading from right to left, show the ones, tens, hundreds, and then the thousands places. When a dial needle is between two numbers, it is the lower number that is read (a needle between 2 and 3 is read as 2).

Before school, read the numbers on the electric meter dials and write them down. The next day, at the same time, read the numbers again and record them. Subtract the second day's numbers from the first reading to find out how many kilowatt-hours of energy your home used over that 24-hour period.

Make a list of the appliances in your home that use electricity from the power company. Saving energy is good for the environment and will save your family money on the monthly electric bill too. How do you think you can use the appliances on your list more wisely to save energy in your home?

Project 18
FOOD ENERGY
The fuel of living things

> **You need**
> - food labels, books, other research materials
> - paper and pencil

For the human body to function, it needs energy. The energy for our bodies comes from the food we eat. Energy from foods is measured in units called calories. Our body changes the calories in the food we eat into energy to grow, maintain itself (stay well), and allow us to use our muscles to do work. In cold weather, the body needs more calories to do its work and also keep us warm.

A person who isn't going to drive very far doesn't need much gas in the car. But for a long trip, a car needs plenty of fuel. In the same way, a person who works at a desk and is not very active will not need as many calories as someone who mixes concrete and carries heavy cement blocks around all day. Some people cut down on the number of calories they eat in order to lose weight. When more calories are taken in than the body needs, it stores the rest as fat, causing the body to gain weight. Fat in the body is stored energy, but too much is not a good thing.

How many calories do you normally consume a day? For one day, list all the foods you eat—don't forget those between-meal snacks!—and how much. Look up how many calories there are in each food and make up a chart. Boxes of cereal and other foods list the amount of calories *per serving*—notice the number of servings per box. Books list the calories in different foods, such as: a ¼ lb. hamburger patty, 224 calories; an orange, 50; ½ cup green beans, 15; an 8 oz. glass of milk, 150; a 6 oz. serving of ice cream, 290; one small chocolate chip cookie, 50. Total up the number of calories you ate during that one day.

Research how many calories a day are healthy for a person of your age and weight. Are you getting too many calories? Are you not eating enough to maintain a healthy body? How could you change your eating habits to cut down or raise the number of calories in your diet and still enjoy what you like?

Project 19

WHEN TO SAY WHEN

Measuring the energy (calorie) value of foods

Our bodies convert the food we eat into energy (see Project 18). Food energy is measured in calories. We need a certain amount of calories as fuel for our bodies, but taking in more calories than we need causes a person to gain weight.

> **You need**
> • research materials

Compare the number of calories in plain foods to the same type of foods that have sugar or something else added to them or are served in a different form. For example, compare the number of calories in a serving of popcorn to a serving of buttered popcorn. Compare the number of calories in a potato to a serving of french fries (or potato chips). Compare the calories in different candy bars that have the same weight. Compare the calories in a serving of peanuts to a serving of honey-roasted peanuts; a serving of whole milk with a serving of chocolate milk. Which foods have more calories?

What ingredients added in the cooking or processing of the foods increase the number of calories in them? By how much—a little, a lot? According to a published health chart, listing calorie needs for your age and weight, are there some foods you should avoid, or limit your intake of?

Project 20
SWEET SEARCH

An examination of sugar, the high-energy food

Foods sweetened with sugar do taste good! Unfortunately, too much sugar hurts our body's ability to use certain vitamins. It makes people gain weight, and causes tooth decay. Some children become hyperactive—that is, they can't sit still—when they take in too much sugar.

You need
- a trip to the supermarket
- pencil and paper

Sugar comes in many different forms: sucrose, glucose (dextrose), fructose (found in fruits), lactose (found in milk), and maltose.

Look at the labels on cereal boxes and compare the amount of calories per serving of cereals that are sugar-coated to those that are not. Usually, the ingredient that is contained in the cereal in the biggest proportion is listed first. Is the number-one ingredient usually sugar, or some form of sugar, in those cereals that are sugar-coated? Which cereals, sugar-coated or non-sugar-coated, do you think are better for your body?

Make a comparison chart showing the cereal's name, the number of calories per serving, and the amount of sugar per serving. Then make a chart comparing calories and sugar per serving of other foods that come in boxes and cans.

Not all labels will list the word "sugar" in the ingredients, even if there is sugar in it, because, as we said, sugar comes in different forms. Research the different kinds of sugar found in our foods. For example, "high fructose corn syrup," a type of sugar, may be one ingredient listed on the label of a can or pork and beans.

Project 21

THE RIGHT STUFF

Seeds store enough food energy for germination

If you were traveling on foot for a long period of time, you would carry a backpack. In the backpack you would store all the food you need to get you to the next camp, where you could replenish your food supply.

In the same way, seeds store just enough energy to be able to grow a root and a leaf. Once a seed has formed a root to gather water and nutrients from the soil and a leaf to collect sunlight, it can begin to make food on its own. The process of a plant making its food by gathering the light energy from the sun is called photosynthesis. Also needed in the process are carbon dioxide, water, chlorophyll (which gives leaves their green color), and very small amounts of minerals. The time from when a seed begins to sprout a root and a leaf (using its own stored energy) until it is able to make food on its own is called germination.

At your local hardware store or garden center, buy 3 different packages of seeds and a small bag of potting soil. The seeds can be flower or vegetable seeds.

You need
- 3 different types of seeds (vegetable or flower)
- potting soil
- a dark place (a closet or basement)
- water
- 3 small containers (plastic drinking cups, etc.)
- masking tape
- pencil and paper

Now, prove that seeds store enough energy to germinate, but then need sunlight to make food in order to continue to grow and live.

Fill 3 small containers with potting soil. Plastic drinking cups or short drinking glasses work well. Get 3 different kinds of seeds; they can be flower seeds (morning glory, marigold, etc.) or vegetable seeds (radish, lima bean, watercress, etc.). Place a piece of masking tape on the side of each container and on each write the name of the seeds you are going to plant in the container. Then put 5 of each kind of seed in their proper container (5 seeds are planted in case some do not germinate). Push the seeds about ½ inch (about 13 cm) down into the soil.

Place the containers in a dark place (a closet, for example) that is at least as warm as room temperature all the time. Water the seeds every day. Keep the soil moist, but not heavily soaked.

Keep a written log of your observations each day. Write down the date and what you see in each container.

Once leaves appear, the stored food energy in the seeds is just about gone, and the plants are ready to begin making their own food. If the plants are kept in the dark and don't get any light to make new food, how long does it take for them to use up their stored energy and begin to die?

If you keep close watch and provide water and light at the right time, the young plants that start withering for lack of food may begin to start getting food from the soil. If not, plant new seeds and give them TLC (tender, loving care), and you may get to see them thrive.

Project 22

IN THE PINK

Home insulation keeps heat in and cold out

When the cold winter winds blow, we need to keep the heat energy from our home's heater inside. Builders use a material called "insulation" to keep warm air inside in the winter and cool, air-conditioned air inside in the summer. Insulation looks like thick blankets of cotton candy, usually pink or yellow in color. It is placed inside walls, ceilings, and sometimes under the floor.

Home insulation is given an "R-rating," which stands for how good a job that particular kind of insulation does. The higher the R-rating number, the better the insulation is at keeping the temperature on one side of the insulation from changing the temperature on the other.

> **You need**
> - 2 shoe boxes
> - adhesive tape
> - clear plastic food wrap
> - scissors
> - 2 thermometers
> - modeling clay
> - a sunny window
> - sheets of Styrofoam (about ½ inch or 1 cm thick)
> - paper and pencil

How do we know that insulating materials do what they are supposed to? Let's prove it.

Remove the lid from a shoe box, or tear the flaps off of another box about the size of a shoe box. Stand the box upright on one end, so it is tall. With scissors, carefully cut a window in the "front" of the box, as shown. The window should be in the upper ⅓ of the box. Then cover the window by taping a piece of clear plastic food wrap over it. Do the same to a second shoe box.

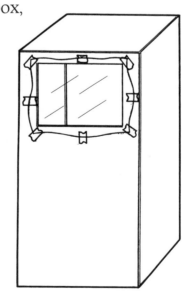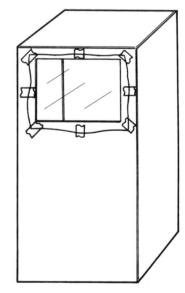

Turn the boxes around to work on the open "back" side.

Styrofoam is a light, usually white material. It is used for many things, including disposable coffee cups and for packing, so that appliances such as TV sets and microwave ovens are not damaged in shipping). It is also an insulating material, inexpensive, which is available in many shapes and sizes at hobby shops and craft stores.

Using adhesive tape or glue, line the bottom half of one shoe box with sections of Styrofoam, covering the three walls and making a "roof."

Inside each shoe box, place a small mound of modeling clay on the bottom. Turn a thermometer upside down and stick it in the clay. Do the same in the other box. The thermometers' bulbs will measure the air temperature inside the boxes.

Cover the open backs of each box with a piece of clear plastic food wrap. Use adhesive tape to make the wrap fit tight.

Place both boxes in a sunny window, with the open "back" side of the boxes facing away from the sunlight. Be sure that the sunlight is not shining directly on the thermometer through the window in the uninsulated box.

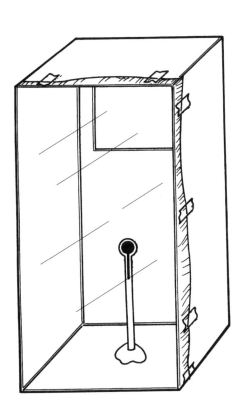

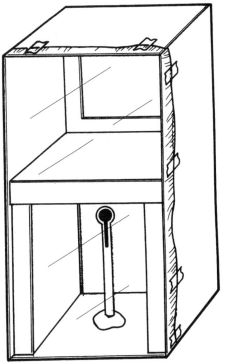

Over a period of one or two hours, take readings and write down the temperature showing on both thermometers every five minutes. Does the air inside the insulated part of the shoe box stay cooler longer than the air in the uninsulated box?

Project 23

KEEPING WARM

Insulating our bodies in cold weather

In the winter, your body needs more energy to keep you warm. We depend on our clothing to insulate us and keep us from losing our bodily warmth to the cold air when we are outside in bitter weather. What type of clothing material makes a good insulator?

Ask an adult to help you gather materials or fabrics to test as insulation. Find as many different kinds as you can. Look through old and worn clothing, that are not much use to anyone (ready to be thrown out, not "handed down" or donated). There

<table>
<tr><td>You need
• small jar
• several different kinds of material (an old T-shirt, towel, jeans, socks, linen, blanket, sweater)
• clock or watch
• warm tap water
• thermometer
• rubber bands
• scissors
• paper and pencil
• an adult</td></tr>
</table>

might already be a bag of rags or scraps stored in a closet. Look over each item for a tag or label that tells what kind of material it is made of. Select several different kinds to test.

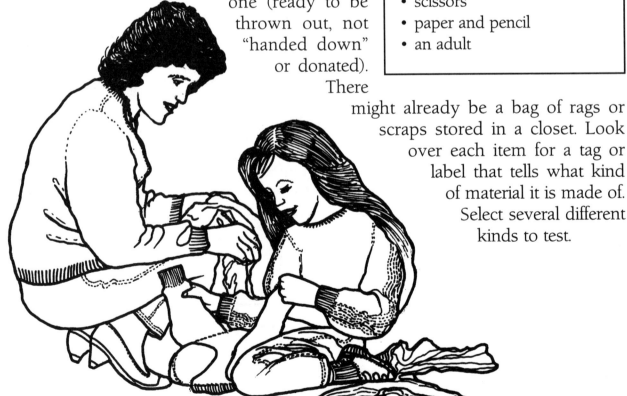

From each different piece of material, cut a square piece of it large enough to completely wrap around the top, bottom, and sides of a small jar (each piece of material should be the same size).

Turn the hot and cold water faucets on in your kitchen sink, and hold a thermometer in the stream. Adjust the faucets until the water is about body temperature (98.6 Fahrenheit/37 Celsius). Fill the jar with this water.

Quickly, stand the thermometer in the jar of water and wrap the jar completely with a piece of material, covering all the sides, bottom, and top. Use rubber bands to hold the material and the thermometer in place—the thermometer sticking up out of the jar.

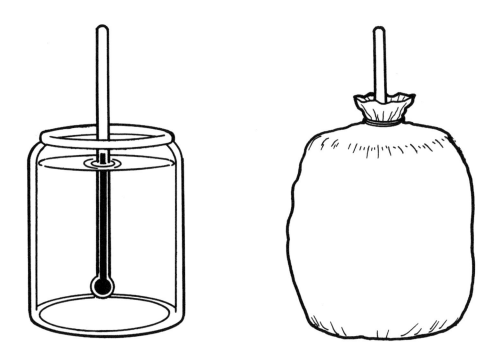

Every five minutes, read the temperature on the thermometer (pull it up slightly if necessary and then slide it back down. Write the temperature down. Continue to record the temperature until it reaches the temperature of the room.

Fill the jar again with body-temperature water, and cover it with a different piece of material. Observe and record the temperature every five minutes until it reaches room temperature. Repeat this procedure for each piece of material you are testing.

(If you have someone to help you, and have more thermometers and same-size jars available, you could test the insulation of several kinds of material simultaneously, at the same time. Just be sure to keep your records straight when you read the temperatures.)

Which piece of material kept the water warm the longest? Do you know what it is made of? Polyester, rayon, cotton, etc.? Can you find out? Which material do you think would be best for making winter clothes? Which would be the worst?

Project 24

SHOCK TREATMENT

Capacitors and the storage of
electrical energy

In the field of electronics, capacitors are components that perform many different tasks in an electronic circuit. One thing they do is temporarily store electricity. Unlike a battery, a capacitor must first be "charged up" with electricity.

Using modeling clay, make a base to hold two 1.5-volt "D" flashlight batteries together. The batteries should be laid down with the positive (+) end of one touching the negative (–) end of the other, just as they would be in a flashlight. The batteries are said to be "in series" with one another. When connected in this way, the total

You need
- 470-microfarad, 35-volt capacitor
- 2-volt T1-size light-emitting diode (LED)
- 2 "D" cell batteries (1.5-volt flashlight batteries)
- 2 insulated jumper leads with alligator clips on both ends
- modeling clay

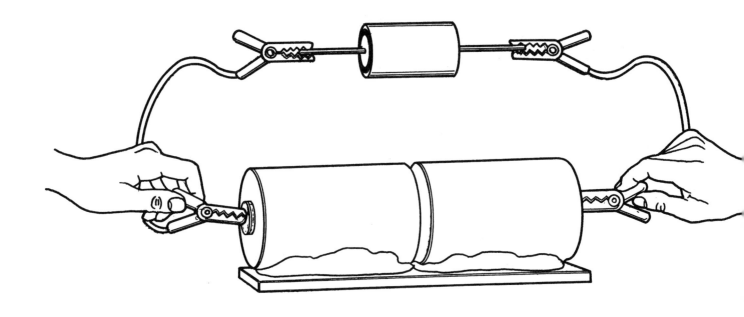

voltage across the two batteries is the sum of each battery: 1.5 volts + 1.5 volts = 3.0 volts.

Connect one end of an insulated jumper lead to one of the leads (wires) coming from a 470-microfarad capacitor. Connect one end of another insulated jumper lead to the other lead coming from the capacitor. Note that batteries have a positive (+) and negative (−) marking on them. Also note that the capacitor also has positive and negative markings.

Taking the unconnected ends of the insulated jumper leads, hold the clip connected to the positive terminal on the capacitor to the positive terminal on the battery. Touch the clip connected to the negative terminal on the capacitor to the negative terminal on the battery for about 15 seconds. The capacitor should be charged.

Now touch the leads from the capacitor to the leads of an LED, a light-emitting diode. While the LED does not have + and − markings, it does have + and − leads, and you must match the + of the capacitor to the + on the LED (and the − lead to the −). You will notice that one side of the LED is a little flatter than the other. The lead that comes from this side is the negative terminal (−).

When you touch the capacitor's leads to the LED, the LED will light brightly for about one second. Then, as it quickly uses up the electrical energy stored in the capacitor, you will see the light very quickly grow dimmer.

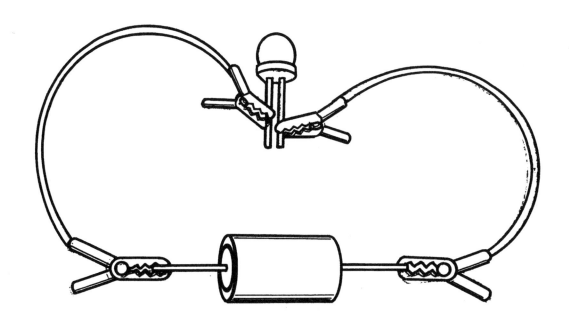

The ability of a capacitor to store an electrical charge is measured in microfarads, abbreviated UF. Would the LED glow brightly for a longer time if you used a capacitor that was rated at more than 470 microfarads?

Project 25
MARBLE ROLL
Converting kinetic energy into potential energy

Energy can be transferred from one object to another. "Kinetic energy" is the energy of an object in motion. If an object is moving and it hits another object, its energy is transferred, or handed over to the other object. On a pool table, players hit a ball with a cue stick, giving kinetic (movement) energy to the ball. When the ball rolls into another ball, all or part of this energy is given to the second ball, and the second ball begins to roll. Even though the first ball may stop, the force of kinetic energy continues on in the second ball.

You need
- marbles
- 2 rulers
- 2 books
- a rug, or carpeted floor
- piece of paper

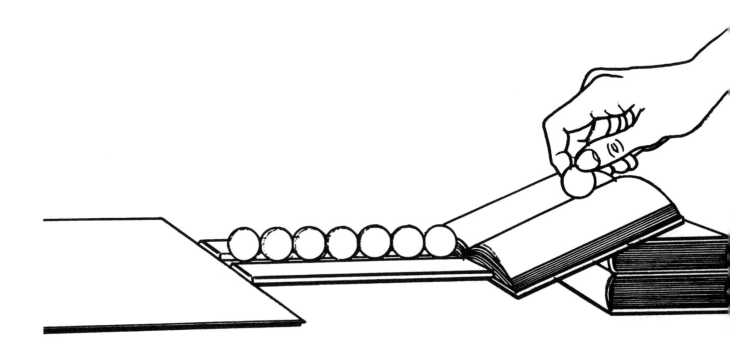

Near a rug, or on a floor that has carpeting on it, lay two rulers next to each other, leaving a small space between them. Lay marbles back to back all along the space between the two rulers. Be sure the rulers are close enough together so that the marbles are not touching the floor—but are being held up by the rulers.

At one end of the rulers, open a book to about the middle. Make a ramp out of the open book by propping up the end opposite the rulers with another book.

Hold a marble at the top of the ramp. Let go. The force of gravity will give the marble motion energy. When the marble hits the first marble on the rulers, it hands its energy over to that marble. Being up against another marble and unable to move, that marble transfers its energy to the next marble. The energy continues to move from one marble to the next until the last marble is reached. When the energy is given to the last marble, it begins to roll, because there isn't anything blocking it. Is there enough energy to knock the last marble off the rulers? How far does it roll? The rug or carpet offers friction to the marble, and helps slow it down. Mark the spot where the marble comes to rest, or stops, with a tiny piece of paper.

Now, remove a few of the marbles so there are gaps between some of the marbles as shown in the illustration below. Roll the marble down the ramp again. Does the end marble roll as far? If not, why not? Do you think it may be because some of the energy was lost before getting to the last marble?

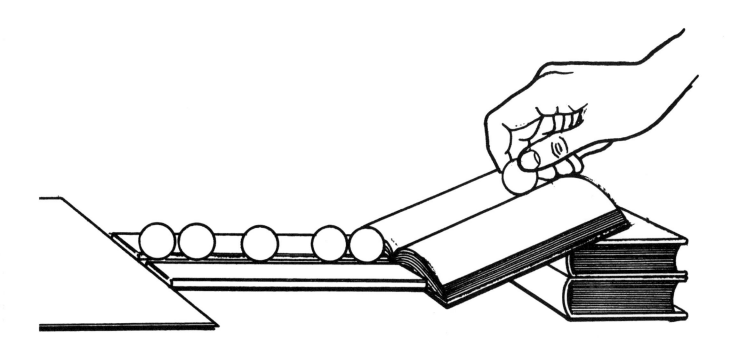

Project 26

FROLICKING IN THE WAVE

How some energies move

Energy can travel in the form of a wave. You are familiar with rolling waves in the ocean. Other types of energy waves, such as sound waves and radio waves, would look similar to ocean waves, if we could see them.

A wave has a "crest" or peak, the highest part of the wave, and it has a "trough" or valley, the lowest part. The length from crest to crest (or trough to trough) is called the "wavelength." The wavelength of a tsunami (a tidal wave) can be 100 miles (161 km) long! The wavelength of a 550 Hertz (cycles per second) sound wave, which is a note that is a little higher than "middle C" on a piano, is 2 feet (60 cm).

<table>
<tr><td>You need
• jump rope
• a fence
• a friend
• eye dropper
• round cake pan
• water</td></tr>
</table>

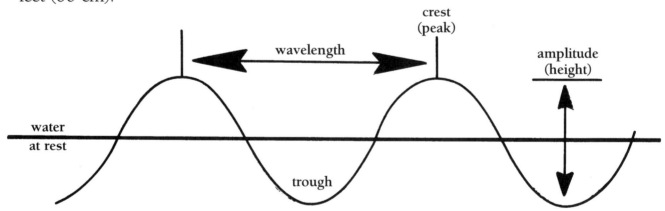

The same thing is true of waves in a lake or an ocean. When you see a rolling wave, it might look like the water is rolling, but very little water is actually moving. The water is only rising and falling as the force of energy passes through it. A boat on the water will bob up and down as the wave energy moves under it. You can demonstrate this by placing a cork or a toothpick in a tub of water and dropping in a stone. The waves created by the stone entering the water will ripple out, and will push the cork or toothpick up and down.

Have a friend hold lightly on to one end of a long jump rope As you hold the other end, quickly whip your end up and down. You will see the rope take the shape of a wave, and travel down the rope toward the other end. If your friend is holding the rope, when the energy gets to his end, it will yank the rope out of his hand.

Now tie one end of the jump rope to a fence. Quickly whip your end up and down, again and again, and set up a wave pattern. If you want to measure the "amplitude" or height of the wave, have a friend stand along side the rope and hold up a measuring stick, and watch where the lowest point (the trough) and the highest point (the crest) fall.

Fill a round cake pan half full of water. Fill an eye dropper with water. You can find the exact center of the pan by squeezing a drop of water into the pan and causing rippling waves. If you squeeze a drop of water perfectly in the center, the waves will ripple out to the edges of the pan, then back again, and meet exactly at the center point. If the waves didn't meet back together, wait until the water calms; then keep trying it until you find the exact center.

Sound wave energy can also travel through other materials besides air. Put your ear on the metal pipe of a chain link fence and have a friend tap a nail on the pipe at the other end. You will hear the sound travel through the pipe.

Project 27

LITTLE SIR ECHO

*Making use of sound waves to
measure distance*

The energy of a sound wave travels through the air at about 1100 feet, or 335 meters, per second. In projects 24 and 25, we saw how energy waves travel through a medium (air, water, metal, etc.) but that the molecules of the medium don't actually travel forward with the wave.

> **You need**
> - a large building
> - tape measure
> - friends

As a rolling wave moves through the ocean, the wave energy moves forward, but the actual molecules of water only move up and down with the wave's crest and trough. That is why a boat on the water will bob up and down, but not move forward, as a rolling wave goes by. This concept can also be shown by tying a piece of ribbon onto the middle of a jump rope, then tying one end of the rope to a fence, and moving the other end up and down, setting up waves. The ribbon will go up and down, but not forward in the direction of the wave.

The energy of sound waves also travels in the same way. Molecules in the air bump into each other and push the wave along, but the actual molecules travel very little.

Since we know that sound travels at about 1100 feet per second, we can use it to determine distance. You are probably familiar with counting "one one thousand, two one thousand, three one thousand," to count the seconds between seeing a flash of lightning and hearing the rumble of thunder. Since 1100 feet is about one-fifth of a mile, a gap of one second between seeing a lightning flash and hearing its thunder indicates that the lighting was about one-fifth of a mile away.

Have you ever gone into an empty room and heard your voice echo off the walls? When your ears hear two sounds that are about one-tenth second or longer apart, your brain interprets those as two distinct sounds...an echo, if the two sounds are the same (a loud yell, for example). Traveling at 1100 feet per second, it takes a sound wave about one-tenth of a second to go 110 feet. If you yell at a large

wall, you will hear an echo if the sound travels 110 feet or more to get back to you. That would mean you are 55 feet from the wall, because the sound would have to travel to the wall and back to you (55 × 2 = 110).

Find a building that has a broad wall, perhaps your school building. Face the wall and stand about 30 feet away from it. Yell loudly at the wall. Take a step backward and yell again. Continue to move back until you hear your voice echo. Then, using a tape measure, measure the distance from the wall to where you stood when you first heard an echo. Is the distance about 55 feet?

Have your friends try it. Record the distance where each friend first hears his echo. Are the distances close to 55 feet? Add the distances together and divide by the number of friends to find the average distance. How close is the average distance to 55 feet?

Project 28

ENERGY UNLEASHED

The hazards of fast-moving water

Many people have built homes on the beach by the ocean. It's a beautiful place to live...until a hurricane comes!

The kinetic energy of moving water can be very powerful. Water moving normally in a river or stream bed usually stays where it should. But large volumes of fast-moving water can overflow the riverbanks, gouging out huge troughs and, like a bulldozer, pushing over cars, houses, and anything in its path.

Set this project up outdoors. Cover an area about 2 by 3 feet (60 × 90 cm) with sand, piling it to a height of about an inch. Make a riverbed in the sand by scooping out a 2 to 3 inch wide (5–7.5 cm) channel from one end to the other of the 3-foot (90 cm) length.

Place some small-scale model buildings along the edge of the "river." Buildings from an HO train set or other small-scale models work well,

You need
• sand
• 4 two-liter plastic soda bottles
• water
• small houses and buildings (scale train-set models, for example)
• large dishpan
• several thick books
• piece of corrugated or stiff cardboard, about 2 by 4 feet (60 × 120 cm)
• plastic food wrap
• adhesive tape
• an area outside

or you can make your own buildings using cardboard and adhesive tape. Also, place some buildings away from the riverbed, making a town.

Cut a 2 by 4 foot (60 × 120 cm) piece of corrugated cardboard from a box (have an adult help you). Fold the piece of cardboard in half, lengthwise–along the 4-foot (120 cm) length. Then open it up again, but not all the way, making a "V" shape. To keep the top of the cardboard from getting wet, cover it with plastic food wrap or aluminum foil. Use tape to hold it in place. The cardboard "V" will be a slope or ramp that will channel water into the riverbed when water is poured into it.

At one end of the riverbed, place the end of the cardboard ramp. Raise the other end of the ramp to a height of about 6 inches (15 cm) by placing several thick books or blocks of wood under it. To keep it in a "V" shape to make a water chute, stack books on both sides.

Fill four 2-liter plastic soda bottles with water. Very slowly pour water out of each bottle onto the high end of the ramp, allowing the water to trickle through the riverbed in the model town. After the bottles are empty, look at the river bed and all the buildings in the town. Write down any changes that you see.

Fill the four bottles with water again. Now empty all of the bottles into a large dishpan. Dump all of the water quickly, at once, down the ramp. The same amount of water now travels through the river as before, but the first release consisted of slow-moving water over a long period of time, and during the second release it is fast-moving water over a very short period of time. Now, when this "flash flood" or hurricane surge of water hits the town, what happens to the riverbed? What happens to the buildings along the river? What happens to the buildings that were not next to the river?

Note: If you have access to a still camera, take "before," "during," and "after" pictures. A camcorder (videotape recorder and camera system) can even capture the live action as it happens.

Do more research into hurricanes, floods, and erosion.

Project 28

SUN, YOU'RE TOO MUCH!

Taming solar energy the natural way

Heat energy from the sun is usually thought of in a good way because of the many benefits. But there are times when this heat is unwanted. Have you ever walked on a beach when the sun made the sand so hot that you had to run or put shoes on your feet? Or gotten into a car "baking" in the hot summer sun with the windows closed up?

You need
- thermometer
- a sunny day
- a large shade tree
- pencil and paper

In winter, bright warm sunshine streaming through the windows of your home helps keep you comfortable inside. But in summer, this *extra* heat causes fans and air conditioners to work even harder, as they try to cool down the house.

Trees can provide natural shading for homes. By planting trees along the side of a house where the hot summer sun beats, a home can be kept cooler naturally, and save electrical energy.

Let's prove that trees lower the temperature of the air in their shade. On a hot sunny day, find a large tree and stand in its shade. There, hold a thermometer out at shoulder height, being careful not to touch the bulb. Wait several minutes for the temperature to settle, then read the thermometer and write down the temperature.

Now, stand in the open, in the sun away from any shade. Again, hold out the thermometer and wait for the temperature to settle. Then read and write down the temperature.

Which location had the lower temperature?

Project 30

THE GREEN SCREEN

Trees as natural wind-energy protection

Protecting a home from strong, cold winter winds would certainly help to keep heat energy inside the house and lower energy costs.

Farms often have large open areas in which acres of crops are planted. To slow strong winds down and protect their crops and topsoil from wind damage, and their homes from cold, farmers often plant trees in a row to grow tall and cut the prevailing winds. Long ago, during long, cold winters, such windbreaks were especially important to the families living in farmhouses, when insulating materials and efficient means of heating weren't as good as today.

Using art and construction supplies or scale models (the kind used for train sets), construct a model of a farm, showing its open crop-filled fields, the farmhouse, and where rows of trees would be placed to act as windbreaks. Research weather maps in the area of your "farm" for wind direction.

Again, using art and construction supplies or models, construct a model of a home or apartment dwelling in a city.

A city home may only have exposure to the wind in the front and back, if it is attached or very close to other buildings on both its sides. Other people's homes or apartments will act as windbreaks for the person's home in the middle.

51

Project 31

CHOOSE NOT TO LOSE

Identifying causes of home heat-energy loss

The wood in your home or apartment's walls and roof, along with insulation material, does a good job of keeping heat inside in the winter and cool air inside in the summer. Wood is a natural insulator. It has millions of tiny cells, sort of like a honeycomb. These cells are natural pockets that trap air, and air does not conduct heat.

You need
- your home
- a windy day
- pencil and paper

Home-building experts say that about 75 percent of a door's heat loss occurs around its edges. That is why people sometimes stuff newspaper or old rags around the edges of an unused door, and push a throw rug against its bottom. Heat energy can also be lost around windows, and electrical outlets and switches.

Investigate your house for places where drafts can enter and rob your house of heat energy. Draw a floor plan of your house, showing where windows, doors, electrical outlets, and electrical switches are located. Then go to each location and check for the presence of a draft. Pay attention to the sensitive soft cheeks of your face; they are a great way to feel moving air. On your floor plan, write down any locations where you feel a draft.

You might see evidence of a draft by holding something light, such as a very small down feather or tiny piece of lint from a clothes dryer's trap, up to where you suspect air leakage.

Have your parents or an adult take you to the local hardware or building-supply store and research ways that would help keep heat from leaking out of these drafty locations.

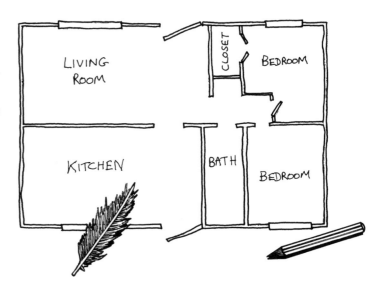

Project 32

NOW YOU HEAR IT...

Tracking radio frequency direction

At radio and television stations, powerful transmitters send radio waves out of the antenna and through the air, on their way to your radio receiver or TV set. Can you use a radio as a direction finder in order to locate the station that a radio wave is coming from?

Take an inexpensive AM pocket radio and place it on the table. Tune it to a station that is coming in strongly and clearly. Fold a piece of aluminum foil in a shape of a cave or pocket and place it around the top, bottom, and three sides of the radio, leaving only the front of the radio showing in the opening. Place the radio back in position on the table.

Is the station still coming in as strong? Slowly turn your radio, along with its aluminum shield, exposing the open front side to different directions. Is the station still coming in as strong? Continue to turn it around until you have made a complete circle. If the station is strongest when facing one particular direction, then that is the direction that radio waves are coming from.

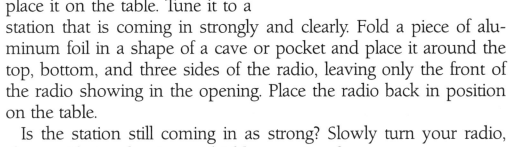

Do the experiment with several other radio stations. Are the signals coming from the same or different directions? List the stations, by their ID letters or where they are on the radio dial, and write down the direction of their signal transmitter.

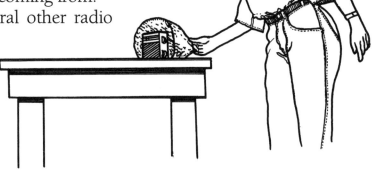

Project 33

ONCE, TWICE, AGAIN

Reusing products to save energy

It takes energy for a factory to make a product. If that product can be used twice, or used to do more than one job, that reduces the need to make more of the product—saving energy.

What items around your home or school can be used more than once, or used in a different way after their first use? Plastic products are often handy to keep for other uses. Responses to a recent consumer poll suggest that 87 percent of Americans had reused a plastic product over the previous six-month period.

SOME ADDED USES FOR MANUFACTURED PRODUCTS

Plastic soda bottles

1. Make into bird feeders.
2. To store cold drinking water in refrigerator.
3. Use as a terrarium.
4. Experiments.
5. A penny bank.
6. Pocket money—return bottles to store for refund.

Can you think of other uses for bottles, and for the other products listed here?

Paper grocery bags

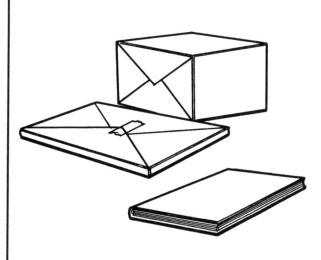

1. Bring to grocery, when out shopping, to pack order.
2. As covers for school textbooks.
3. To carry things, such as gifts, when visiting relatives.
4. To wrap packages for mailing.
5. For arts and crafts projects, such as masks for plays or Halloween.
6. Spread out to protect work area.
7. Place them in your community's recycling trash pickup.

Plastic margarine tubs

1. To store screws or small items.
2. To store food leftovers.
3. As scoop—for dog food, animal feed, fertilizer.
4. To catch water under small flower pots.
5. With puncture holes in bottom to sprinkle water on plants.
6. As beach toys, to hold sand and water, or use as molds for sand castles.

Plastic grocery bags

1. Line small bedroom wastebaskets.
2. To carry school lunches that may be soggy or might leak.
3. To put carried books or packages in when it starts to rain.
4. When packing a wet bathing suit.
5. To hold wet laundry to hang or dry.
6. To keep feet, or shoes, dry in rainstorm.
7. To collect recyclables for pickup.

TIP: Stuff each bag, one by one, into the top of an old stocking and cut a hole in the toe to make a handy plastic bag dispenser!

Project 34

UNPLUGGED!

Taking home electrical use for granted

The development of electrical energy has been a wonderful benefit to mankind. But society has become very dependent on electricity. Sometimes the power coming into our homes is interrupted. We take the many things that work by electrical power for granted—until the power is lost! This

can happen when there is trouble with the electric utility equipment, lightning strikes a telephone pole, strong storm winds blow down power lines, or too many people simply use too much electricity all at once or for too long. Then, the lights can *go out*!

Losing electric power to a home means that many things we normally do, without giving them much thought, suddenly become inconvenient. Some things are only small inconveniences, such as using candles or flashlights instead of electric lights for a few hours. You may not be able to watch your big-screen TV, but you can still read, play a game, or listen to a battery-operated radio.

However, the loss of electrical power can cause serious problems. If the power fails during the winter and your home is warmed by electric heat, a loss of electricity could make the house uncomfortably cold. If your home has its own water well, an electric water pump cannot work without power. The kitchen sink is not normally thought of as being electrical, but if the water pump is out, you can't bring water into the pipes; so there is no water for drinking, cooking, washing, or for flushing a toilet. No water can be a very serious problem.

What things around your home would stop working if the electric power should go off? What things around your home use energy but are not connected to and dependent on the electric utility company? Examples would be a candle, a wind-up toy, a flashlight, a watch, and a kerosene lamp. Can any of these items be used to replace an item that uses electric power from the power company, and save electricity? A wind-up clock could replace an electric clock; it would require you to wind it up every day, but that would save electrical energy. However, a battery-operated radio would not efficiently replace a radio that runs on house current, because batteries are more expensive.

Project 35

TREASURE HUNT

Your neighborhood with/without electrical power

When Thomas Edison and his team of scientists perfected the electric light bulb long ago and began building electric stations to generate power, towns and cities took on a whole new look.

Walk down your street or around your neighborhood and imagine what it would look like without electrical energy. What would be missing? Would you see streetlights? Flashing traffic signals? How about those bright, neon signs in storefronts? Television antennas? People lined up at bank ATM machines? A fire box? Satellite dish? Telephone poles? Transmission towers?

Make two drawings, one showing what your street or neighborhood looks like and another of what the same scene would look like if electricity had not been developed.

Project 36

LOOKING UP

Most of Earth's energy comes from our sun

Almost all energy on the Earth comes from the sun's energy (geothermal, tidal, and nuclear are the only ones that do not).

Wind is caused by the uneven heating of the Earth's surface by the sun. Waves in a large body of water can be the result of winds. Wood, used for many things including firewood to heat homes, comes from trees, which require sunlight to grow.

Oil products (coal, gas, oil, kerosene, and propane) are formed by rotting plants and wood, packed down tightly and under great pressure for many centuries.

The energy of moving water in streams is partly caused by the sun's energy. Rivers, streams, and waterfalls are the result of evaporation caused by the sun's energy. The water then falls back to Earth as rain, snow, or some other form of precipitation, and gravity moves it from a higher to a lower level.

Electrical energy for our homes is generated at a power plant often by burning a fossil fuel such as coal. Hydroelectric power is generated by water moving through great turbines.

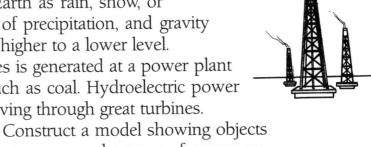

Construct a model showing objects that represent the types of energy on Earth that directly or indirectly are the result of solar energy.

Project 37
NUCLEAR DOMINOS
Demonstrating a chain reaction

One type of energy is released when the nuclei of atoms are either combined (fusion) or split apart (fission). The energy, called "nuclear energy," is released in the form of heat, light, or some other type of radiation. Nuclear energy is used to make electricity by heating water for steam that then drives giant turbine generators.

> **You need**
> • dominos
> • ruler
> • flat table

In the process of nuclear fission, the splitting apart of an atom causes a chain reaction. A radioactive element, such as Uranium-235, is used in the chain reaction. The first fission creates two new neutrons. Each of these neutrons strikes at least two other neutrons, which strike even more, and a chain reaction takes place which continues to grow.

To demonstrate the concept of nuclear fission, stand dominos in the pattern shown, where one domino is set to start a chain reaction. As it falls, the domino hits two dominos, which each hit two more. The number of dominos hit and falling with each row grows quickly. This chain reaction of falling dominos can be demonstrated easily using only 4 or 5 rows; with additional rows the arranged dominos become so packed together that they get in each other's way.

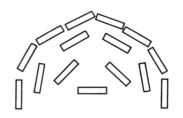

In a nuclear reactor where nuclear fission is taking place, the chain reaction can be slowed down or even stopped by inserting rods made of cadmium or boron. These dampening rods absorb neutrons and slow the process down. Demonstrate this by placing a ruler between two dominos in a row, then push the first domino to start the chain reaction. The reaction stops when it reaches the ruler, which acts like the rods in a nuclear reactor.

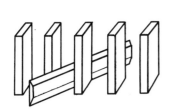

Project 38
ENERGY STOPPER
Friction and the reduction of energy

Friction is a force that can act on a moving object to slow it down, requiring the use of additional energy if it is to be kept going. Friction is caused by two objects rubbing together. When you are ice skating or riding a sled down a snowy hill, friction tries to reduce your rate of motion. The metal runners on skates and sleds are specially designed to reduce friction so that you are able to go faster.

To demonstrate friction and how it can rob energy, cover a piece of cardboard about 1 foot (30 cm) square with clear plastic food wrap. Pull the food wrap tightly across the cardboard and use adhesive tape underneath to keep it tight. Take the cardboard outside and lay it on a flat surface, such as a driveway or sidewalk.

Place a dry bar of soap in the middle of the board. Hold one end and slowly raise it, making a ramp, until the bar of soap begins to slide. At this point, the force of gravity is stronger than the friction. Place the zero-marked end of a ruler or measuring stick on the flat surface and hold its scale markings against the high end of the cardboard ramp. Write down how many inches or centimeters high it had to be to overcome friction.

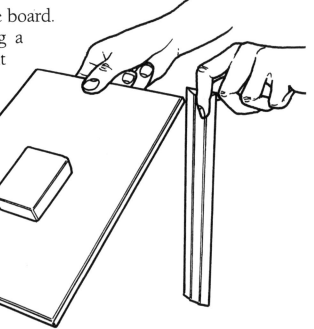

You need
- clear plastic food wrap
- adhesive tape
- bar of soap
- water
- cardboard, about 1 foot (30 cm) square
- ruler, yardstick, or meter stick
- a flat surface outside (sidewalk, driveway, porch, etc.)
- pencil and paper

Next, thoroughly wet the bar of soap and pour water onto the cardboard ramp. A watering can would work well for this job. Will water reduce the friction?

Place the bar of soap at the exact spot where it was before, at the middle of the ramp. Lift the end of the ramp until the bar of soap overcomes friction and begins to slide. Measure the height of the ramp. Did the ramp have to be raised as high, before the soap moved the second time?

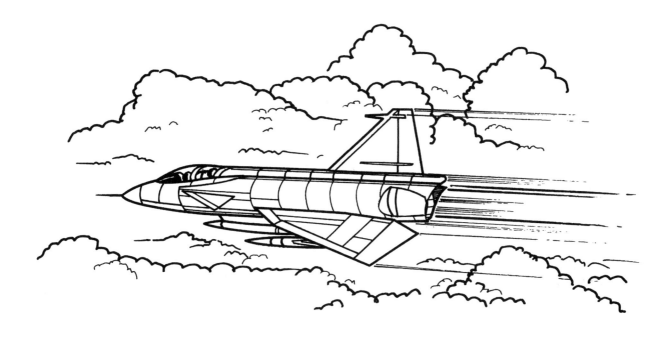

Moving through the air causes friction, too. It can increase the energy usage of cars, planes, and other vehicles—which is why they are designed to be as "aerodynamic" as possible. Do more research on how friction can be an energy robber.

Project 39

CELL MAGIC

Changing light energy to electrical energy

The photovoltaic cell, better known as a "solar cell," is a device that turns light directly into electricity. Solar cells are expensive to manufacture, so they are only used when there is no other easier way to get electricity, such as at a remote weather station or in an Earth-orbiting satellite.

A single solar cell does not generate very much electricity, but solar cells can be connected together "in series" and their individual voltages added together. Connecting cells in series means hooking the positive (+) terminal of one cell to the negative (–) terminal of the next. Flashlights have their batteries connected in series, with the negative terminal of one battery touching the positive terminal on the next. When batteries are connected in series, the total voltage available across all of them is the sum of the individual battery voltages as shown. Imagine how much more power you could exert on a rope if the strength of three of your friends were also helping you to pull it.

Using insulated jumper leads with alligator clips on each end, connect the positive and negative terminals of a solar cell to a small 1.5-volt hobby motor. Set the

> **You need**
> - 3 hobby solar cells (delivering about ½ volt each)
> - small DC hobby motor (requiring 1½ to 3 volts direct current)
> - insulated jumper leads with alligator clips on each end
> - a sunny window with a shade, blinds, or curtain
> - several small wooden blocks

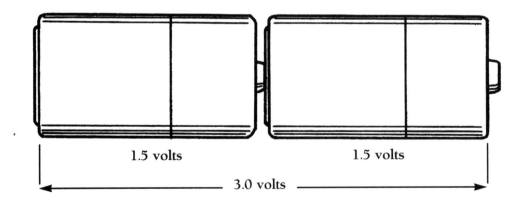

1.5 volts   1.5 volts

3.0 volts

arrangement in a sunny place. Use wood blocks behind the cells to tilt them so that they face the sun. You could also use spring-type clothespins clipped onto the sides near the bottoms of the cells to stand them upright. Watch how fast the motor spins. Next, add two more solar cells to the circuit, placing them in series.

Look at and listen to the motor. Is it spinning faster now that it is getting more voltage? What happens to the motor's speed on a cloudy day?

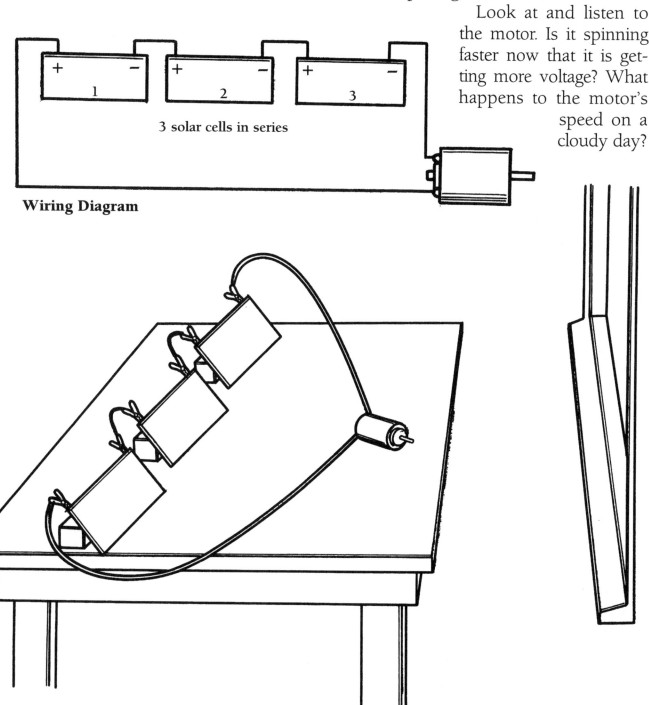

3 solar cells in series

Wiring Diagram

Create your own "cloudy day" by closing blinds or curtains partway, then all the way. Do you think the voltage produced by the solar cells is less on cloudy days? How do you think that affects the location of where solar cells work best?

Project 40

HEAT LOST?

Using energy to remove (transfer) heat

The invention of the refrigerator has been a tremendous benefit to people, keeping foods from spoiling quickly. When the refrigerator runs, what happens to the air inside it? Where does the heat go? It doesn't just disappear. The refrigerator actually moves it out into the room.

<table>
<tr><td>You need
• 3 thermometers
• refrigerator
• string</td></tr>
</table>

To cool the air inside a refrigerator, another energy source is needed—electricity. Tubes inside the refrigerator are filled with a fluid called "refrigerant." It absorbs heat. With the help of an electric motor, the heated fluid goes through a "condenser" and the fluid gives up its heat to the surrounding air. The condenser is made up of coils and is found either on the back of your refrigerator or at the bottom. If you don't see the coils behind it, look under the refrigerator.

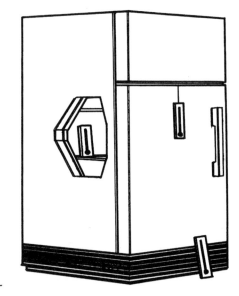

Put a thermometer inside the refrigerator. Place another near the condenser coils, wherever they are on your refrigerator. Tie a piece of string to a third thermometer and hang it on the front door, about in the middle, to measure the room temperature.

Wait for the refrigerator's condenser motor to turn on, which it will do occasionally when the temperature inside the refrigerator rises above the temperature that its thermostat is set at. Listen for the motor to stop in a few minutes. When it does, read the temperatures on all of the thermometers. Is the temperature near the condenser coils warmer than the room temperature shown on the thermometer hanging on the door?

Air conditioners use the same principle. If you have a window air conditioner running, try placing a thermometer inside it and one on its outside. Is the heat from the room being moved to the outdoors?

Project 41

BRIGHT HEAT

Unwanted heat energy from incandescent light

The most common types of home lighting are incandescent and fluorescent bulbs. In both, electrical energy is turned into light energy.

In an incandescent light bulb, electricity passes through a small wire, called a filament, which glows brightly. In a fluorescent light bulb (usually a long straight or circular tube), the inside of the bulb is filled with a gas. The inside glass of the bulb is coated with materials called phosphors. When electricity is passed through a heating element in the bulb, the gas gives off rays that cause the phosphors to fluoresce (glow).

You need
- light from a fluorescent tube
- light from an incandescent bulb
- thermometer
- pencil and paper
- an adult

All we really want from a light bulb is light. However, in the changing of electrical energy into light energy, there is energy loss. Some of that energy is given off as heat, especially unwelcome during hot weather! Which type of light bulb is more energy-efficient (gives off less heat to the surrounding air)?

Find a lamp in your home that uses an incandescent bulb; most lamps do. Find a fluorescent lamp. In the home, fluorescent bulbs are often used in kitchens, bathrooms, garages, and workshop areas. Remember, when working around hot light bulbs and electrical fixtures, to have an adult with you. A light bulb may stay quite hot even after it has been turned off, and it can cause a burn—so be careful. Also, do not take bulbs out of their sockets.

Remove the shade from a lamp that has an incandescent bulb. Hold the bulb of a thermometer about one inch (2.5 cm) away from the lit bulb for about three minutes. Record the temperature.

Now hold the thermometer bulb the same distance from a lit fluorescent bulb for three minutes. Record the temperature. Which bulb is more light-efficient?

Project 42
UNEQUAL ENERGY
*Finding the distribution of heat energy
in a room*

Is the temperature in a room the same every-where in the room? You might think that it is. But as you do this project, you may be surprised to discover that the air temperature is different in different parts of the room—the heat energy in the room is not equally distributed.

Pick about ten different locations in a large room in your home. Some locations should be

You need
- a large room in your house
- thermometer
- a clock or watch
- paper and pencil
- an adult

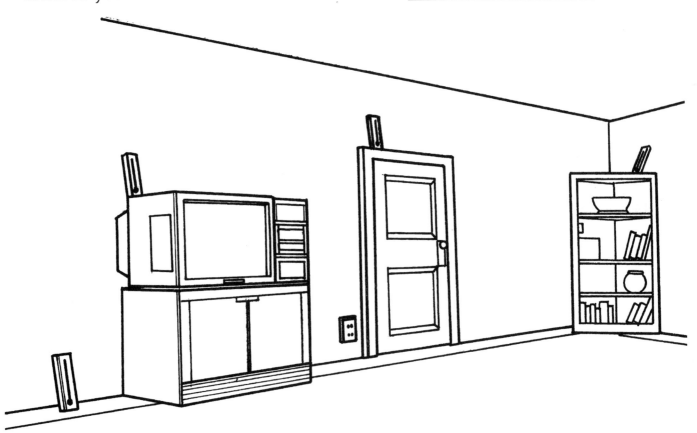

high up, some low near the floor, some on an "inside" wall (a wall with another room behind it), and some on an "outside" wall (with the outdoors on the other side). High locations can be above an inside door (over the open doorway or, with the door ajar, the thermometer lying on top) or on top of a picture frame on a wall. Ask an adult to help you place thermometers in the highest places. One of the locations should be by a window, another by an electric light switch on an outside wall.

Make a chart with two columns and at the head of the first column write "locations"; then list the locations you've selected. At the top of the second column write "temperature."

Put the thermometer at your first location. Wait about three minutes to give the thermometer time to adjust and indicate the correct temperature. Write down the temperature reading for that location. Repeat this procedure for all of the locations in your room.

Compare the temperatures you have taken around the room. Which location is the warmest? Which is the coolest? Why do you think the temperature may be different at each location? Look up the word "convection" in the dictionary. Do you think poor insulation by a light switch on an outside wall or by a window might be affecting the air temperature at that location?

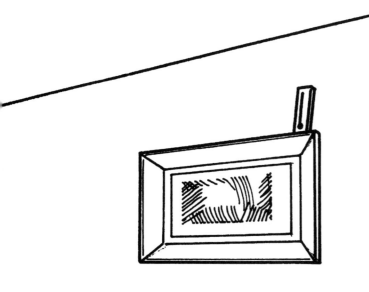

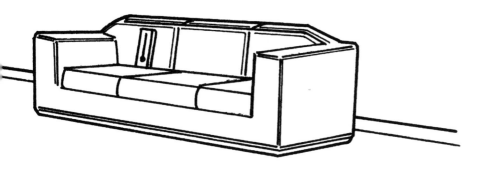

Project 43

BAND AT TENSION

Measuring potential energy in a stretched elastic band

When you pull the elastic band of a slingshot back as far as it will go and hold it, the elastic band has potential (stored) energy, ready to do work. When you let go, that potential energy is released to do work. This energy in motion is called kinetic energy.

How can we show that the more a rubber band is stretched, the more potential energy it has (and the more kinetic energy is released when you let go of the rubber band)?

Let's construct a paper towel tube "cannon" and use a Ping-Pong ball as a cannonball to measure kinetic energy when it is shot out of the cannon. Don't use anything heavier as the cannonball, because flying objects can be dangerous. A Ping-Pong ball is safe to use.

Take two pieces of masking tape about 4 inches (10 cm) long. Lay them on top of each other, with sticky sides touching..

Fold the masking tape over one end of an empty paper towel roll. Position it so that it covers only a part of the paper towel roll opening as shown. Use another piece of masking tape to hold it onto the roll. This tape will act as a "stopper" by making the opening just small enough to keep the ball from falling through, but will let it stick out of the bottom a little. Lay the roll aside for now.

Using masking tape, tape a ruler to a piece of wood about 3 or 4 inches (8–10 cm) wide

> **You need**
> - Ping-Pong ball
> - masking tape
> - empty paper towel roll
> - thick book
> - measuring tape
> - rubber band
> - board, about 3–4 inches (8–10 cm) wide and 1 foot (30 cm) long
> - ruler
> - 2 nails
> - hammer
> - paper and pencil

by 1 foot (30 cm) long. Let about 5 to 6 inches (13–15 cm) of the ruler hang over one end of the board.

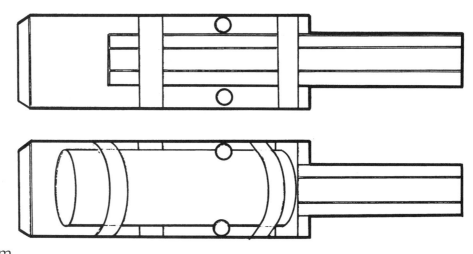

Hammer two nails part of the way into the board, one on each side near the outside edges, about 3 inches (7.5 cm) from the end of the board where the ruler is. Leave the nails sticking up slightly.

Lay the paper towel roll on top of the ruler and board assembly, between the nails, and fix it in place with masking tape. Set your "cannon" on the floor.

Elevate the front end of the cannon by placing a book under the end opposite the ruler. Put a rubber band across the two nails, stretching it around the bottom of the paper towel tube. Drop your "cannonball" into the tube so it comes to rest at the bottom of the tube, on the masking-tape stopper and the rubber band.

Using the scale on the ruler, pull the rubber band back 1 inch (2.5 cm) and let go. The rubber band will hit the ball and shoot it out of the cannon. Watch where the ball first touches the floor. Use a tape measure to find the distance the ball traveled out of the cannon. Make a chart to record how far back the rubber band is pulled and how far the ball travels through the air.

Next, pull the rubber band back 1½ inches (4 cm). Measure and record the distance the ball travels. Repeat this procedure, ½ inch (1 cm) at a time, until the rubber band has been stretched back as far as it can.

Look at your chart of data. Does the ball travel farther if the rubber band is pulled farther back? Is there a mathematical relationship (a number pattern) between the distance the rubber band is pulled back and the distance the ball goes? For example, does the ball go 1 foot (30 cm) farther for each inch (2.5 cm) the rubber band is pulled back?

Project 44

LESS THAN BRIGHT

Brownouts in electric power service

The demand for electrical energy by those living in our cities and communities changes constantly. For example, on very hot summer days, more people use fans and air conditioners, so the demand on electricity from the power company is higher.

What happens if a 10-megawatt power plant tries to deliver 10½ megawatts during a time of such high demand? A power company may choose to lower the voltage going out a little, so there is enough to go around to everyone. This is called a "brownout." A power plant representa-

tive told us that when demand for electricity goes higher than the plant can produce, the power company can reduce power by 5, 10, or even 15 percent. Most people won't even notice a 5- or 10-percent reduction in power.

In a really bad situation, when more electricity is needed than even a brownout can help with, the power plant may have to turn power off to different areas, each area losing power for 15 minutes at a time. This is called a "rolling blackout." By losing power for only 15 minutes, most people are only slightly inconvenienced.

When a brownout occurs, the normal voltage available to the electrical appliances in your home is reduced. In lamps during a brownout, light bulbs may not shine as brightly as normal.

Although running a light bulb at a lower voltage will not harm it, lower voltages for a long period of time can damage motors. To make up for the voltage drop, a motor will draw more current. The increased flow of electricity through the motor's "windings" (coils of wire inside) makes the wire heat up. This can destroy the motor. Motors can be found in many places around the house: refrigerators, water pumps, air conditioners, swimming pool pumps, fans, and forced hot-air heaters all have motors. If a brownout occurs at your house, alert an adult to turn off appliances until the power returns to normal.

To get a taste of a brownout, in this project we will operate a flashlight bulb at only ½ the voltage it is designed to take and compare it to a bulb getting full voltage.

Using modeling clay, make a base to hold two 1.5-volt "D" flashlight batteries together. The batteries should be laid on a small board or piece of cardboard, with the positive (+) end of one touching the negative (−) end of the other, just as they would be in a flashlight. The batteries are said to be "in series" with one another. When connected in this way, the total voltage across the two batteries is the sum of each battery: 1.5 volts + 1.5 volts = 3.0 volts.

Clip one end of an insulated jumper lead to the small metal tip of a flashlight bulb. Clip one end of another insulated jumper lead to the wide metal base of the bulb. Touch the other two ends of the jumper leads to the batteries as shown.

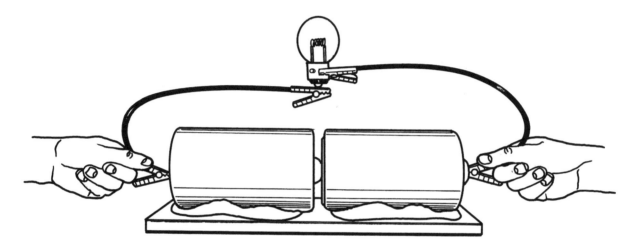

Make another identical setup, but this time only use one battery. Compare the brightness of the two bulbs.

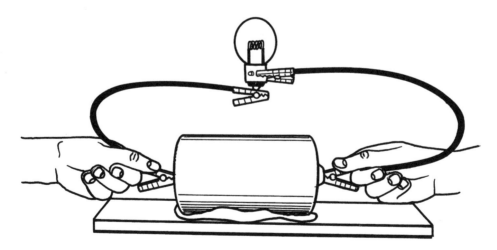

Call your local electric power company and research more information about brownouts and blackouts.

Project 45

ENERGY DETECTIVE

Helping your school save energy

When energy is used inefficiently by your school, it not only wastes valuable resources, it also costs your family, neighbors, and community money by increasing the school's expenses. Is your school conserving energy? Do an investigative study and give your school a report on its use of energy.

Start your investigation by talking to one of your school's custodians or maintenance people. Ask about the insulation in the school's walls and ceiling, how old the insulation is, if it is miss-

ing or damaged in some areas, if there is enough insulation. Ask the custodian about the heat and light in classrooms after everyone goes home. Is someone in charge of turning the heat down and making sure unnecessary lights are turned off at night? Are the heating and lighting on timers? Ask if the mechanical and electrical equipment in the school is in good operating condition. Do your own physical inspection of the school building. Ask yourself such questions as:

- Are there a lot of windows in the school? Are they on the side of the building that allows warm solar energy to come in during the winter? Are there shades to keep out the hot summer sun?
- What direction do the prevailing winds come from? Does the school building receive any protection from cold winds, as from other buildings or large trees?
- On windy or cold days, are there drafts around windows and outside doors?
- Are some rooms hotter than they need to be (in winter) or cooler than they need to be (in warm weather)? Use a thermometer to measure the temperature in rooms you feel are too warm or cold.
- Are there dripping or leaky faucets, or long or constantly flushing toilets in the rest rooms? Ask a friend of the opposite sex to help you check for such water waste.
- Is the water coming from the faucets so hot that it might scald someone? If so, the thermostat on the hot water heater may be set too high.
- Do the exhaust fans in the kitchen run unnecessarily?

Interview one or more teachers and ask them what they do to make their classroom more energy efficient. Do they store and use paper, books, and other materials wisely? Do the windows in their classrooms let in enough natural light so that the teacher can turn off some of the electric lights during the day? Are computers, printers, and other electronic equipment turned off when not in use?

Interview a local builder or architect and ask for ideas on improving the energy efficiency of your school building.

Study the data you have collected and compile an energy report for your school. Include suggestions for improvement. Obviously, there will be some things you cannot change, such as the efficiency of the school's boiler. But you can ask teachers to assign a student to see that the lights are turned off when everyone leaves the room for recess or for lunch.

Most trash from schools is paper. Instead of throwing out paper that is only used on one side (old flyers and printed reports), ask teachers about making use of the other sides for scribbling notes or as scrap paper in classes. The school can also set up places where everyone can deposit used white paper for recycling.

You may want to enhance your report by taking photographs. Show and report on both good and bad points about your school building.

Project 46

WINDY CORNERS

Comparing available wind energy

Someday our homes may not need to be connected to electrical power lines for energy. Newly constructed or redesigned housing, with solar cells and efficient windmills, will perhaps in the future be able to gather energy and produce enough power to fill the needs of the families living there.

If you were thinking of installing a small windmill where you live, where around your house would be the best place to set it up? Usually, windmills are mounted very high up, in order to catch the strongest wind. But suppose you had to mount one on the ground. Where, on the ground, do you think the wind is strongest? Is it windier in the middle of the side wall of your house, or at the corners?

To find out, make a device to measure wind strength. Push a thumbtack into the eraser end of a pencil. Tie a piece of thread about 10 inches (25 cm) long onto the thumbtack.

> **You need**
> • a house
> • pencil
> • thumbtack
> • thread
> • pencil and paper

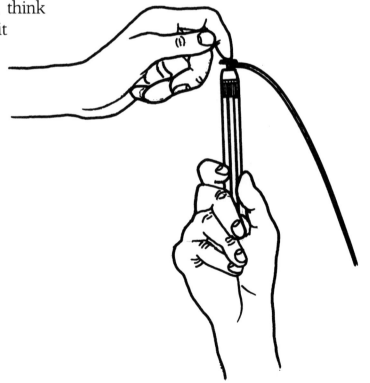

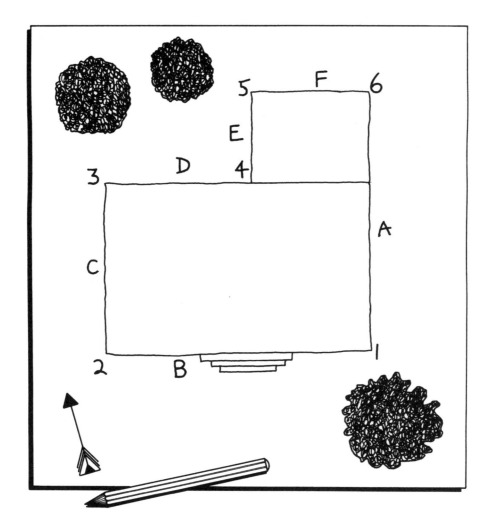

Make a sketch, or rough drawing, of the layout of your house, as it would be seen from overhead. On the drawing, label each side: A, B, C, and so on. Label each corner: 1, 2, 3, in the same way.

Go outside and stand in the middle of each side wall and at each corner of the house. At each position, hold the pencil straight up and at arm's length, to catch whatever wind there is. The windier it is, the greater the angle the thread will be from the pencil. Is it more windy along the broad sides of your house or at the corners?

Check the effect of the wind every day for a week (some days will be more windy than others). Is it true that the corners (or the sides) are always windier? Why do you think that is?

Project 47

ENERGY ATTENDANT

Changing energy-wasteful habits in your home

Can you help make saving energy a way of life for the people you live with? Using seat belts has become a good habit for many adults because their children nagged them every time they got into the car—the children having been taught about seat belt safety at school.

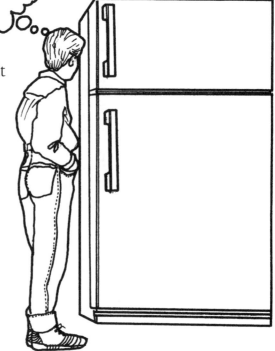

Before saving energy becomes a habit in your house, you will have to be on the alert for times when energy is being wasted and politely point it out to your family. Maybe you can change these energy-wasting patterns for the better, and make energy saving something your family does automatically, as routinely as getting up in the morning, eating breakfast, brushing teeth, and heading out for school or work.

Make a list of the ways your family can save energy, and give them a copy to remind them. Everyone should be happy to help, because they can all take part and saving energy will also save them money.

Some Simple Energy-Saving Ideas

- Before opening the refrigerator door, think about what you need. Then open the door, quickly get the items you want, and close the door. Every time a refrigerator door is open, heat from the room goes in, and the refrigerator must work to cool that warm air. It's a good idea to place often-used products (milk, eggs, butter, cheese) in the same place in the refrigerator so they can be found easily and time is not wasted searching.
- Turn off lights when a room is unoccupied.
- Televisions, computers, and radios should be turned off—*if* no one intends to use them within a half-hour. These appliances receive a lot of wear and tear when they are first turned on, so it's better to leave them on, for up to a half-hour, if you or someone will be using them within that time.
- Toast two slices of bread at the same time, instead of first one slice and then another a minute later. Toasters, like other electrical heating devices, use a lot of electricity.
- Encourage the use of a microwave oven to cook, whenever possible. Microwave ovens use about 50 percent less energy than conventional ovens.

Project 48

CHECK YOUR GAME

The energy cost of electronic fun

Before electricity was available in every home, families and friends entertained themselves by playing games using cards, boards, dice, "men," marbles, and other objects. With the invention of electricity and new advances in electronics, the world of games has really changed, with all kinds of computer and video games now filling store shelves.

Some games now available on home computer used to be played without using electrical energy. Card games like solitaire and board games like Monopoly, for example, are just two games now popular on computers that can still be played in the "traditional" way, saving energy.

How many games do you have that need energy to play them (don't forget battery-operated ones)? How many games do you own that do not require energy?

> **You need**
> - pencil and paper
> - research
> - electric power company bill (optional)
> - television set, video computer game console, computer (optional)

78

Make a list of the games that can be played both with a computer and without (start with solitaire, chess, and Monopoly). Visit game and computer stores to find more computerized versions of traditional card and board games for your list.

"Playing" with higher math, older students may want to try calculating how much energy (and money) can be saved by playing games that do not require electricity. Here's how to do that.

To determine the cost of using an electrical appliance, look for a label or tag on the unit or refer to the owner's manual to find its power consumption. The power consumption figure will be listed in "watts." Electric power companies charge by how many "kilowatt-hours" are used. One kilowatt is equal to 1,000 watts. It takes one kilowatt-hour of energy to operate ten 100-watt light bulbs for one hour (10 × 100 = 1,000).

To find out how much energy it takes to play a TV video game, look on the back of the television set and on the video game console for the power consumption of each, listed in "watts." Add the two numbers together. Let's assume that the video game uses 50 watts and the television set uses 150 watts. That makes a total of 200 watts. To convert this to "kilowatts," a unit the power company uses, divide 200 by 1,000, which equals 0.200 kilowatts. Have an adult search out a recent electric bill and help you determine how much it costs for 1 kilowatt-hour of power. You can get a rough idea by dividing the amount due on the electric bill by the number of kilowatt-hours used that month. This information will be listed on the electric bill.

Suppose your electric bill was $165.13 and the kilowatt-hours used was 1,365. Dividing $165.13 by 1,365 equals 0.12, or 12 cents per kilowatt-hour. So, to play the video game for one hour would cost about 0.200 times 12 cents, or 2.4 cents. It may not sound like much money, but just think of how many hours a year you and your family spend playing that video game! Calculate how much it does cost you for a year!

To find how much energy it takes to play a computer game, remember to add the power consumption of both the CPU (the "central processing unit," or main part of the computer) and the monitor, since both are needed.

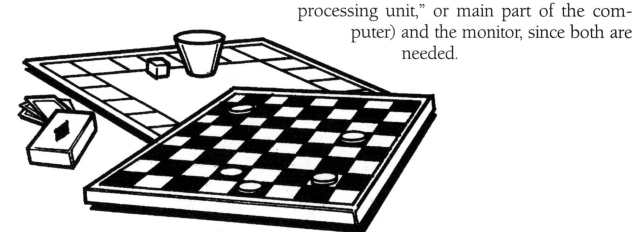

Project 49

HEAT WAVE

Discovering how microwaves generate heat

Microwaves are a kind of radio frequency energy (electromagnetic waves). Their frequency (the number of times the wave vibrates each second) is much higher than most other types of radio and TV waves.

Microwaves are used for telephone and satellite communications, and for fast cooking. When microwaves pass through food, they cause the molecules in the food to move back and forth very rapidly. This generates heat. Have you ever rubbed your hands together rapidly to warm them? A microwave oven works in a similar way. Microwaves vibrate the molecules of water, sugar and fat in food, but pass right through glass, pottery, paper, wood and plastic. That is why, although food cooks in a microwave oven, the dish doesn't get hot—except for some heat transfer from the food. Metal blocks microwaves, so should never be used in a microwave oven.

You need
• use of a microwave oven
• 2 thermometers
• coffee or tea cup (must be "microwave safe")
• water
• an adult

Can you prove that a microwave oven does not cook by making the air in the oven hot, like a traditional oven does, but by heating up the food from the inside?

Ask an adult to help, and fill a cup with water. Put it inside a microwave oven and heat it for 60 seconds. Be sure the cup is "microwave safe," that is, made of plastic, glass or pottery without any metal in it or metallic decorations on it.

When the time is up, take the cup out of the oven. Lay a thermometer inside the oven and close the door (but DO NOT turn the oven on). Stick a thermometer into the cup of water. After about two minutes, take the thermometer out of the oven and compare it to the one from the cup of water. Does the thermometer that was in the water read a higher temperature than the one placed in the oven?

Project 50

NO TAN WANTED

Cold-blooded animals and heat energy

Animals gather energy from the sun to warm their bodies and maintain their normal life processes. Even turtles, which are cold-blooded animals, sit for hours on rocks along a pond "sunning" themselves. A captive snake is sometimes seen standing straight up. It does this to get more light on its body to warm itself. Iguanas need heat to properly digest their food. Grasshoppers cannot chirp if the temperature falls below 62 degrees Fahrenheit (17° Celsius).

Research cold-blooded animals that must have warming energy from the sun in order to live. Draw or construct a scene showing how these various animals gather warmth from the sun.

Project 51

STATIC INTERFERENCE

Detecting sources of stray radio frequency energy

One kind of energy that we can't see or hear is called radio frequency energy. Radio frequency energy is formed by electromagnetic waves that travel through the air. Radio frequency energy allows us to communicate with one another. It is used to bring TV pictures and sound to our homes from stations far away. Two-way radios let people talk to each other from remote places (you may even own a pair of "walkie talkies"). Cordless telephones allow people to talk on the phone while walking around the house or going outside without being restricted by a wire connecting the handset to the telephone base.

You need
- electric shaver
- cordless telephone
- fluorescent light
- electric blanket
- electric hair dryer
- AM radio
- personal computer
- television
- paper and pencil

"Cellular phones," both hand-held and car phones, permit communications with people who are not near a regular telephone. All of these types of communication are possible because of an invisible kind of energy called radio frequency energy.

Some things may give off radio frequency energy, even when we don't want them to. Things that have electric motors often produce radio frequency energy when they are working. This energy may be unwanted, since it can interfere with other things that use radio frequencies, such as TVs, radios, and cordless telephones.

What things around your home do you think might be radiating (giving off) radio frequency energy? How about an electric shaver, a fluorescent light, an electric blanket, an electric hair dryer, an AM radio, a personal computer, or a television?

Since we cannot see or hear radio frequency energy, we will use a radio as a detector to help us find things around the house that are producing radio frequency energy.

Tune a portable AM radio to a spot on the dial where no station is heard. Bring the radio close to each of these objects:

- an electric shaver
- a fluorescent light (often found in the kitchen or bathroom)
- an electric blanket
- an electric hair dryer
- a personal computer
- a television (turn the volume down on the TV set)

Write down your observations about each appliance. Did you hear a sound in the radio? If so, describe the sound; was it a crackling sound or a humming sound?

Call a friend on a cordless telephone. Ask your friend to be quiet and listen. Then hold your phone close to each of the appliances listed above, asking your friend each time what she or he hears, if anything. If your friend has a cordless phone, it's your turn to listen. What do you hear?

What other things around your home or school can you check out as radio frequency producers? What do you think—which makes the better radio frequency detector, an AM radio, or a cordless telephone?

Project 52

GREAT BARRIER ICE

Magnetism vs. water and ice

Magnetism, an invisible form of energy, can go through air. Can it go through water? What if the water is in the form of ice, where the molecules are in a more orderly and structured form. Does it affect magnetism?

Fill a long, cylindrically shaped balloon with water. Don't inflate the balloon, just fill it with water in its uninflated shape. Tie the balloon to the middle of a pencil. Lay the pencil across two cups or glasses to let the balloon hang down.

Lay a book on either side of the cups, so that they are separated by the balloon. On one book place a staple, and on the other, a strong magnet.

With the water-filled balloon between the staple and magnet, move staple and/or magnet until they are just close enough to each other that the staple is captured by the magnetic force of the magnet. Note the spot where the staple first showed signs of being attracted by the magnet. Measure the distance between the magnet and this spot.

Without disturbing the books or the magnet, move the cups, with the pencil and balloon in place, to the freezer. Keep the setup the same, so the balloon will have the same shape as when the ice was water. When the water in the balloon has frozen, remove the setup from the freezer and put it back by the books.

Place the staple back on the book opposite the magnet at the spot where it was first attracted to the magnet. Does the force of magnetism go through the ice and move the staple? If it does, is there any difference in the distance between the staple and the magnet before the magnetic attraction affects the staple?

You need
- strong magnet
- staple, from stapler
- two cups or glasses
- two books
- pencil
- cylindrically-shaped balloon
- use of a freezer
- ruler

Project 53

ONWARD AND UPWARD

Transferring energy uphill

Can a wave of energy travel uphill? We learned, in Project 25, that energy travels in the form of a wave, and moves forward even though the objects passing the energy along do not. (They *may* move, but only a short distance compared to that of the energy transferred.) But uphill…?

Place two dominos under a ruler to make a sloping ramp. Stand a domino on the ruler with its broad sides facing the ends. If the standing domino falls over, remove a domino under the ruler. If it stays standing, try to add another domino to make the ramp even steeper. Add dominos under the ruler until the ramp is as steep as possible without the upright standing dominos on top falling over. When you have made the ramp as steep as you can, stand a line of dominos along the ramp. Space them about 1 inch (2 cm) apart.

Push on the top half of the first domino, on the lowest part of the ramp, and tip it forward into the next-higher one. Does a chain reaction occur and 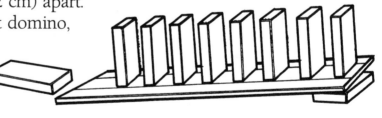 knock the top domino off the ruler? If so, a wave of energy, which came from your "push," traveled uphill, even though the actual domino you pushed only moved a little bit.

To do more experimenting with this project, you may want to try making a wave of energy go even more steeply uphill. You can do this by building steps with building blocks, or other materials, and again using dominos to try to transfer the energy uphill. With steps, the dominos can stand on a level surface; but remember that to make the next domino in line fall forward, it must be hit on its top half. If it is struck near the middle or its lower half, it could fall backwards instead of forward.

Project 54

INVISIBLE BEAMS

Locating light in the darkness

Some kinds of energy are invisible. A beam of light energy itself is invisible. We see light only when the light energy directly enters the eye, or reflects off an object and bounces into the eye.

Normally, we can't see the light rays that are coming from the sun (*never look directly at the sun*) but only see the things the sunlight shines on. At dusk, after the sun has set where you are, you may have noticed the sun's light shining brightly on an airplane flying overhead. High in the sky, the airplane is still being hit by the sun's light energy rays, even though you can no longer see the sun from Earth's surface.

You may also have seen sunbeams, when the sun's light streams through a break

<table>
<tr><td>

You need
- flashlight
- small cardboard box
- scissors
- talcum powder
- a dark room
- an adult

</td></tr>
</table>

in the clouds. Because there are billions of tiny dust particles in the air, it's possible to see the sun's light energy bouncing off them against a dark sky beyond. Other times, after a rainstorm, the water droplets in the atmosphere behind us, away from the setting sun, will reflect the sun's light at different angles and show you a rainbow. Sunlight also contains other types of invisible energy rays that we cannot see. In the summer, you cannot see the ultraviolet rays coming from the sun, but too much of this kind of energy will give you a sunburn!

To make light rays visible, have an adult help you cut a small hole about the size of a large coin in a small cardboard box (a shoebox would work well). Turn a flashlight on and place it inside the box so that its light shines out through the hole. Close up the box so that the hole is the only place where light can escape from inside.

Place the box on a table or dresser in a very dark room. Standing several feet in front of the box, gently shake or squeeze some talcum powder from its container into range of the light energy coming out of the box. The light from the flashlight in the box can now be seen bouncing from the powdery talcum particles.

A light beam can also be a useful tool, helping us to see particles in the air that are normally too small for us to notice or see well. Instead of using talcum powder, if you have them try clapping two chalkboard erasers together. You can also shake a fresh facial tissue, right from a box, into the beam. Try different brands of facial tissue. Do some give off more lint particles than others?

Project 55

PENNY SHOOT

Newton's law and the transfer of energy

Sir Isaac Newton, an early scientist born in England in 1642, formulated the physics laws of motion. His first law of motion states that "an object at rest tends to stay at rest, and an object in motion tends to stay in motion." A famous trick demonstrates this law. A playing card is placed over a drinking cup and a coin is laid on top of the card, directly over the mouth of the cup. Then the edge of the card is given a sharp tap with a finger or pencil.
The blow knocks the
card off the cup,

You need
- section of wood, 3 or 4 inches (8–10 cm) wide by about 2 feet (60 cm) long
- five coins
- a smaller coin
- two nails
- hammer
- small rubber band
- stapler
- thin cardboard
- scissors
- smooth paper

but the coin on the card, being at rest, stays in position. Then gravity pulls down on the coin and it drops into the cup.

Let's build a device that will not only demonstrate this law of Newton's, but also show transfer of energy (energy from one object being handed off to another object).

Cut a strip of smooth paper to fit on the wooden board. Towards one end of the board, hammer two small nails, spaced about 3 inches (7.5 cm) apart, partway into the wood. The nails should be sticking up out of the wood about an inch (2.5 cm), looking like goal posts at a football field.

Stretch a small rubber band between the two "goal post" nails. Cut a small strip of thin cardboard, about an inch (2.5 cm) wide by two inches (5 cm) long. Fold it in half around the rubber band (in the middle) and staple the cardboard ends together. Push the rubber band down on the goal posts, so it rests almost against the wood.

About one inch (2.5 cm) in front of the goal posts, place one of the medium coins face up. Then stack four more of the coins on top, but with tails up.

Grab the stapled piece of folded cardboard between your thumb and index finger and pull back. A stretched rubber band is said to have "potential energy," energy that is stored up and ready to do work.

While the rubber band is stretched, place the smaller coin between the goal posts. Release the cardboard so that it strikes this coin and shoots it towards the stack. The idea is to knock the bottom coin out from under, leaving the other four stacked coins at rest (although they will drop straight down due to gravity).

You may have to try this several times. Your aim may be off, and sometimes the smaller coin may fly slightly upwards and miss hitting the bottom nickel. If a coin does move from the stack, it may happen too fast for you to see. To be sure it was the *bottom* coin that really was knocked out, see if the coin that was moved has heads or tails up. If it's heads, then you successfully shot out the bottom nickel.

This project also shows two examples of the transfer of energy. When the stretched rubber band (potential energy) is released (kinetic energy), energy from the rubber band is transferred to the smaller coin, giving it motion. Energy is then transferred again when this coin hits the stacked coins. The force must be great enough for this struck coin to overcome the friction of the coins on top of it—and the surface under it, which is why we placed a piece of smooth paper under the stack.

The "momentum" of the moving coin will determine just how far it will travel after it has been shot out from under the pile. Remember, "objects in motion tend to stay in motion," so once the nickel is moving, it will *naturally* try to keep going; friction eventually slows it down enough to make it stop.

WORDS TO KNOW

A science glossary

assumption When doing a science experiment, scientists often make assumptions that certain things are true. An assumption is something that is believed to be true. In Project 1 of this book, a glass of a light-colored soda and a glass of a dark-colored soda are used to find in which glass an ice cube will last longest if the glasses are placed in sunlight. The experiment is to learn the difference caused by sunlight on color, but it assumes that the differing contents of the dark and the light sodas (fruit juice, carbonation, sugar, sugar replacement) have no effect on the melting of the ice cube.

calories For the human body to function, it needs energy. We get energy for our bodies by eating foods. The amount of energy we can get from a particular food is measured in units called calories.

capacitor an electronic component used in television sets, computers, radios, and other electronic devices, which performs a variety of tasks. Capacitors can temporarily store electrical charges.

centrifugal force a force that pushes outward when an object is moving in a curve

drag an aviation term meaning the resistance by air to the forward motion of an aircraft. Drag is a force that tries to slow a plane down as it moves faster through the air, causing it to use more fuel energy.

fluorescent bulb (see "incandescent bulb")

frequency With regard to radio waves, the "frequency" of an electromagnetic wave is the number of times it "vibrates," or "cycles," per second.

friction the resistance to motion when two things rub together. Rub your hands together briskly and friction will cause you to feel warmth. Sometimes friction *is* desirable, such as when you are trying to walk on ice. Melting ice reduces friction, making ice very slippery!

centrifugal force

germination the time between when a seed begins to sprout a root and a leaf (using its own stored energy) and when it is able to make food on its own

gravity a force of attraction between two objects

hypothesis a thoughtful, reasoned guess about something, based on what is known. A hypothesis must be proven by experimentation.

incandescent bulb The most common types of electric lights used in our homes are incandescent and fluorescent bulbs. In both kinds of light, electrical energy is turned into light energy. In an incandescent light bulb, electricity passes through a small wire, called a filament, which glows brightly. In a fluorescent light bulb (which is often in the shape of a long, straight tube or a circular tube), the inside of the bulb is filled with a gas. The inside glass of the bulb is coated with materials called phosphors. When electricity is passed through a heating element in the bulb, the gas gives off rays which cause the phosphors to fluoresce (glow).

kilowatt-hour a unit of measure of electrical power consumption used by power companies in determining how much to charge their customers for the electricity they use. A kilowatt is 1,000 watts. It takes one kilowatt-hour of electrical energy to operate ten 100-watt light bulbs for one hour.

LED, or light emitting diode an electronic component that produces a small light from a semiconductor material. LEDs are commonly used in watches and as light indicators on home stereos, computers, and other home electronic appliances.

magnetism a force by certain objects which attracts iron

mass how much "stuff" an object is made of. The more mass it has, the heavier it is. A Ping-Pong ball and a golf ball are about the same size and shape, but a golf ball has more mass.

microfarad a unit of measure of electrical storage used to indicate how much of an electric charge can be stored by an electrical component called a capacitor

microwaves Microwaves are a kind of radio frequency energy. They are electromagnetic waves. Their frequency (the number of times the wave vibrates each second) is much higher than most other types of radio and TV waves. Microwaves are used for telephone and satellite communications as well as for cooking in "microwave ovens."

nuclear energy is a type of energy that is released when the nuclei of atoms are either combined together (called fusion) or split apart (called fission). The energy released, called "nuclear energy," is in the form of heat, light, or some other type of radiation. Nuclear energy is used to make electricity by heating steam that drives giant turbine generators.

observation using your senses—smelling, touching, looking, listening, and tasting —to study something closely, sometimes over a long period of time

photosynthesis The process of a plant making its food by gathering light energy from the sun is called photosynthesis. Also needed in the process are carbon dioxide, water, chlorophyll (which gives leaves their green color), and trace amounts of minerals.

radio frequency energy electromagnetic waves used to carry TV and radio signals

trajectory the path of an object as it travels through the air

trajectory

wavelength Energy can travel in the form of a wave. You are familiar with rolling waves in the ocean. Other types of energy waves, such as sound waves and radio waves, would look similar to ocean waves, if we could see them. A wave has a "crest," or peak, the highest part of the wave, and it has a trough, the lowest part. The length from crest to crest (or trough to trough) is called the "wavelength." The wavelength of a tsunami (a tidal wave) can be 100 miles (161 kilometers) long! The wavelength of a 550 Hertz (cycles per second) sound wave, which is a note that is a little higher than "middle C" on a piano, is 2 feet.

windbreak an object that reduces the force of the wind. Trees are sometimes planted around a house to act as a windbreak, protecting the house from strong winds.

Index

About the Authors

BOB BONNET, who holds an Master's Degree in environmental education, has been teaching science at the junior high school level for over 25 years. He was a State Naturalist at Belleplain State Forest in New Jersey. Mr. Bonnet has organized and judged many science fairs at both the local and regional levels. He has served as the Chairman of the Science Curriculum Committee for the Dennis Township School system and is a Science Teaching Fellow at Rowan College in New Jersey. Mr. Bonnet is listed in *Who's Who Among America's Teachers*.

DAN KEEN holds an Associate in Science Degree, having majored in electronic technology. Mr. Keen is the publisher of a county newspaper in southern New Jersey. He was employed in the field of electronics for 23 years and his work included electronic servicing as well as computer consulting and programming. Mr. Keen has written numerous articles for many computer magazines and trade journals since 1979. He is the coauthor of several computer programming books. For ten years he taught computer courses for adults in four schools. In 1986 and 1987 he taught computer science at Stockton State College in New Jersey.

Together, Mr. Bonnet and Mr. Keen have had many articles and books published on a variety of science topics. They are the author of the books *Science Fair Projects: Environmental Science*, *Science Fair Projects: Electricity and Electronics*, and *Science Fair Projects: Space, Flight and Astronomy*—all published by Sterling Publishing Company.